Studies in the Gospels

Alan Jenkins

Grosvenor House
Publishing Limited

The right of Alan Jenkins to be identified as the author of this
work has been asserted in accordance with Section 78
of the Copyright, Designs and Patents Act 1988

The book cover is copyright to Alan Jenkins

This book is published by
Grosvenor House Publishing Ltd
Link House
140 The Broadway, Tolworth, Surrey, KT6 7HT.
www. grosvenorhousepublishing. co. uk

A CIP record for this book
is available from the British Library

ISBN 978-1-83615-291-0
eBook ISBN 978-1-83615-292-7

DEDICATION

I dedicate this book to all those young men and women who were instructed and introduced to the Gospel of Christ by their presence at the Christian camp, on the Gower peninsular, over the many years of gospel witness and happy fellowship. May the Lord continue to prosper His word and ways in their lives.

ACKNOWLEDGEMENTS

1. J. A. Alexander – A commentary on the Gospel of Mark – The Banner of Truth Trust
2. Kriss Akabusi – On your mark – Studies in Mark's Gospel – The bible reading Fellowship
3. William Barclay – The Gospel of Mark – The daily study bible The Saint Andrew press – 1954
4. J. G. Bellet – The Evangelists – Meditations on the Four Gospels – Pickering & Inglis
5. Alva J. McClain – The greatness of the Kingdom – BMH Books – 1959
6. J. Heading – The Servant Son – Gospel Tract Publications – 1990
7. Theological Wordbook of the Old Testament – Moody Publishers – 1980
8. W. E. Vine – Expository Dictionary of New Testament Words – Oliphants – 1940
9. J. N. Darby – Synopsis of the books of the Bible – Matthew – John – Morrish –

INTRODUCTION:
PRECEPT – GOSPEL STUDIES

The production of this book is the result of a series of Gospel addresses given over a period of time, to a regular congregation of believers and non–believers, in an evangelical outreach. It presents the claims of the Gospel of |Jesus Christ, as depicted in the writings of each of the gospel writers.

This study of the gospels departs from the conventional approach of verse by verse analysis and seeks to focus on the salient features of recorded events, though not in order of occurrence. The studies in Mathew and Luke are similar in structure with suggestions for further investigation on set themes.

The gospel of Mark is different in structure with suggestions in each chapter for sermons or lessons delivered that illustrate the main theme of the gospel ie, the servant of in action.

The last of the studies in John's gospel takes the characters referred to in various chapters and looks at those features that stand out in encounters with the Lord Jesus Christ and the outcome in each case, I trust that these studies will prove profitable to those who would undertake such study and lead to a greater appreciation of our gracious Saviour.

OUTLINES IN THE GOSPEL OF MATTHEW

MATTHEW – CHAPTERS 1 & 2

THE BIRTHDAY OF THE KING

(1) Progeny – Genealogy – Son of David/Abraham – v's 1 – 17
(2) Problem – conception – Unmarried – The Holy Spirit – v's 18–24
(3) Place – Bethlehem – Of Judaea – As promised Ch. 2 v 3
(4) Pursuit – Magi – where is He born King? ch. 2 v's 1 – 12
(5) Plight – Lamentation – A voice heard in Ramah verse 18
(6) Providence – Take the child into Egypt – God v's 13 – 18

    (i)   Progeny – Genealogy

The birth of a king is always an event of particular importance for a nation, the birth of the King of kings is therefore of greater importance. In the genealogy given by Matthew in his record, particular notice must be given to the names of Abraham and David chapter 1 verses 1, 2, & 17; verse 6 informs us that David was the anointed head of the Kingdom, the true line of Messiah's throne, and Abraham was the depository of the promise in whom all the families of the earth should be blessed, thus the two are named together.

    (ii)   Problem – conception

The penalty for Mary, in her situation, was death, according to the law. The angel appealing to Joseph prevented this, as Joseph, so instructed, to 'fear not' to take Mary to wife.

(iii) Place – Bethlehem
The place of the birth of Jesus was predicted in the prophecy of Micah (see Micah ch. 5 vere 2) some 700 years before it took place. This being brought about because of the edict of the Roman Emperor to carry out a census, requiring Joseph and Mary to travel to Behtlehem.

MATTHEW – CHAPTER 3

THE BAPTISM OF THE KING

(1) The kingdom at hand – The preaching – v's 1 – 10
(2) The kind of fruit – Repentance – v's 11 – 12
(3) The king who is Mighty – The one who comes – v's 13 – 15
(4) The kingship declared from Heaven – My beloved Son v's 16 –17

   (i) The Preaching
   Matthew tells us that John came 'preaching in the wilderness' – 'Repent for the Kingdom of Heaven is at hand' thus fulfilling the words of Isaiah 'the voice of one crying in the wilderness' (see Isaiah ch. 40 verse 3) The expression 'kingdom of Heaven' appears in Matthew only and is in relation to Israel; Christ will rule supreme in this kingdom which is universal and shall not be destroyed..

   (ii) The 'fruit' produced prior to the establishment of the Kingdom is that of 'repentance' 'preached both by John and the Lord'

   (iii) The one who comes, mightier than John, is our Lord Jesus Christ, with a ministry that far exceeds that of John, and encompasses a future judgement executed by Christ as indicated by verse12.

(iv) The voice of John proclaiming the coming of the Lord was in fulfilment of prophecy, as written, but another voice of greater import was heard on this occasion as the Father declares identification with His Son, and indicates His pleasure in the obedience of His Son to the Father's will.

MATTHEW – CHAPTER 4

THE INTRODUCTION
TO THE KINGDOM

(1) The temptation of the King – The tempter came –
v's 1 – 11

(2) The Light of the Kingdom – Light is sprung up –
v's 12 – 17

(3) The preaching of the Kingdom – From that time –
v's 18 – 22

(4) The gospel of the kingdom – Galilee of the gentiles –
v's 23 – 24

(5) The people of the Kingdom – From Galilee, Decapolis etc,
v 25

    (i)   The temptation of the King ——— THE LEADING
Many have asked 'Why this temptation'?
Whatever view is taken, one thing is clear, 'Christ
was the sinless one' and this temptation was to
prove 'so it was'. It was real in the Saviour's
experience, but victory over sin and Satan was the
outcome. He was in all points tempted like as we
are. Yet without sin (Hebrews ch. 4 v 15)

    (ii)   Light of the Kingdom – Light is sprung up ——— THE
LIGHT
The people who sat in darkness 'saw a great light'

Once again Matthew uses a quotation from scripture Isaiah chapter 9 verses 1 –2 to demonstrate that Christ is the Light of the Kingdom (see also Isaiah ch. 42 v 6)

John chapter 1 v 9 – The true light —— which lights everyone etc.

(iii) The preaching of the Kingdom – From that time —— THE LESSON

Jesus is now, having waited for the testimony of John to close, able to preach that the 'kingdom of heaven' is at hand. Jesus, when commissioning the twelve, and sending them forth, says to them, as you go, preach the 'Kingdom of heaven' is at hand (see Matthew ch. 10 v 7).

(iv) Gospel of the Kingdom – Galilee of the Gentiles— THE LANDS

The quotation from Isaiah ch. 9 v 1 is clearly an indicator of the preaching of the Kingdom to the gentiles in the resurrection of Zebulun and Naphtali. Zebulun is the representative of Israel having intercourse with the gentiles for profit.

(v) The people who followed Jesus and listed in verse 25 —— THE LISTENERS chapter 4 and they came from Decapolis, Jerusalem, Judaea and beyond Jordan. Persons had been attracted from 'all quarters'. The nature and scope of the ministry of the Lord is depicted in verses 23 – 25

MATTHEW – CHAPTER 5

THE MAGNA CHARTER OF THE KINGDOM

The blessed of the Kingdom – Principle
The blessed:

(i)   Poor in spirit – spirit of self deprecation
      Spirit of man – self confidence —— HUMILITY

(ii) Those that mourn – Holy sorrow ——— HURT

(iii) Physical sorrow – circumstances – as set against
      Strife, divisions, hate, —— HINDERANCE
      The meek Self assertion in man's eyes – self
      submission is God's requirement.

(v)   The seeking righteousness – evidence of New Life
      HEARTFELT
      Keynote of soul satisfaction – Fullness is the key
      'Seek first the kingdom of God and His righteousness'
      (all these things will be 'Added') The beatitudes:
      Blessings on those with features that are pleasing to
      God.
      The Merciful – God's mercy endures forever' – such
      will find mercy. No salvation without 'Mercy'.
      Pure in heart – Absolute purity is God's – Christ
      produces 'purity' in the believer – 'Purity puts God's'
      glory above everything else.

The peace makers – Strife, divisions, hate, works of the flesh, discord etc should not mark God's children. God is essentially
A God of 'peace'. Jesus said "Peace I leave with you"
The persecuted – ie. For righteousness – this the Lord endured – Look at the reason why? His desire to be found in the 'will of God'

(vi) The disciples.
You are the 'salt of the earth', the 'light of the world'
Witnesses against the iniquity that prevails in the world.
Good salt cannot help giving a 'wholesome flavour'.
Unobscured light cannot help shining.

MATTHEW – CHAPTER 6

THE LAWS OF THE KINGDOM

(1) Treasures of the earth – corruption – Open to thieves
(2) Treasures in Heaven – Secure – nothing to corrupt
(3) Rich in faith
(4) Reaching for the Kingdom

(i)   Treasures on earth – where does the heart lie? — EARTHLY
The act of giving should be done in secret where only God can see and give due reward in a coming day. Do not let your left hand know what your right hand is doing. This is further applied to prayer and fasting.

(ii) Treasures in Heaven – A single eye for the eternal rather than the temporal. Do not store for yourself treasures on earth, store for yourself treasures in heaven for where your treasure is there will your heart be. ——— ETERNAL

(iii) Do not worry about your life, God will provide, the exercise of faith is exhorted as God provides for His creation in all phases of life. Richness in faith will honour His name. ——— EVIDENCE

(iv) Seek 'first' His kingdom and all these things will be given, therefore do not worry about tomorrow for tomorrow will look after itself. ——— EXECUTE

(iii)   We are to be 'Rich in good works' (see 1 Timothy ch. 6 v 18). Also 'Rich in faith' (see James ch. 2 v 5) and partakers of the unseen riches of Christ (see Ephesians ch. 3 v's 8 & 10)
These will produce 'heavenly treasure'. ──── EFFECT
You cannot serve God and mammon.

(iv)   Reaching for the Kingdom
Seek first the Kingdom of God and His righteousness !! – Priority in Life.
Take no thought for your life! It is the will of God that His children should live without worry or anxiety. He who has 'saved' us will care for us (see 1Peter ch. 5 v 7; Based on Psalm 55 v 22). Take no thought for the morrow for the morrow will take thought for the things of itself. God prepares us for this seek to please him today. ──── EXERCISE

MATTHEW – CHAPTER 7

THE INVITATION TO THE KINGDOM

(1) Entry to the Kingdom
(2) Requests relating to the Kingdom
(3) Fruit in the Kingdom
(4) Standing in the Kingdom

    (i)   Entry to the Kingdom – REGULATION
Enter in at the strait gate. Character and conduct are supreme in those who have entered by the 'Strait gate'
Thus the chapter begins with the Lord setting up the 'standard of judgement'.
No man is to be 'his brothers judge'
There is great danger in a 'suspicious, judicial spirit', self examination should precede such.
Judgement of present and evident evil in a situation that requires discipline, but carried out with a spirit of reconciliation.

    (ii)   Requests relating to the Kingdom. – REQUESTING
Ask ad it will be given you, seek and you shall find, knock and it shall be opened; requests will be granted from the Father to those who ask Him in faith. So in everything do to those what you would have them do to you.

(iii)   Fruit in the kingdom – REPRODUCING
        False prophets – by their fruit you shall know them.
        Every good tree bears good fruit and every bad tree
        bad fruit.

(iv)   Standing in the kingdom. – RELIABILITY
        Not everyone who says "Lord, Lord" will enter the
        kingdom, only those who do the will of My Father.
        Everyone who hears My words and puts them into
        practice is wise and will be on a firm foundation,
        those who do not so will be unwise with a
        foundation that cannot stand and will fall with a
        great crash.

MATTHEW – CHAPTER 8

THE MANIFESTATION
OF THE KING

(1)   The will of the King – I will be clean
(2)   The great faith commended – Not even in Israel
(3)   The cost of following the King
(4)   The Authority of the King
(5)   The recognition of the King

    (i)   The will of the King ——— WILLINGNESS
The leper represents Israel (Unclean)– The cleansing touch was needed, the whole of Israel was like the leper
The prophet Isaiah speaks of the moral state of Israel and things had not changed. Now the God of Israel was in the land and the priest would be a witness to His power in the healing of the leper, but rejection would still be the outcome.

    (ii)   The great faith commended ——— WITNESS
The insertion of this event by Matthew is apt in view of the previous event, since the centurion was a gentile and yet exercised such faith as to warrant the commendation of the Lord. God shows his grace to the gentile when the children of Abraham were to be left blind for a season

(iii)   The cost of following – Jesus was sleeping in the boat – don't you care that we are 'perishing'. How far from the truth?

(iv)   The Authority of the King —— WORD
These words of mine, and puts them into PRACTICE I will liken to a wise person.

(v)   The recognition of the King – WAKEFUL
The demon possessed men were overwhelmed by the presence of Jesus, so much so, that the demons cried out, "have you come to torture us before our time"? The Lord accommodated their request, sending them into the swine, the reaction of the community was to request His departure, not realising the impact of such in regard to His person and ultimate judgement.

MATTHEW – CHAPTER 9

THE COMPASSION
OF THE KING

(1) The palsied man – The question of 'forgiveness of sins' – verses 1 – 8
(2) Matthew – Jesus calls Matthew – He leaves his occupation
(3) John's disciples and fasting – The bridegroom
(4) Jairus's daughter – Not dead but sleeping–+++++++
(5) Woman who touched His garment – Your faith has healed you
(6) Two blind men – '' do you believe I am able to do this?
(7) The harvest – plentiful – The labourers few.

There now follows another company, made up of individuals, who benefits from the power and compassion of the Saviour.

  (i) The palsied man —— FORGIVENESS
       The Lord deals with this man in his own city; The city had witnessed many of His mighty miracles, and had been exalted to heaven. (see Matthew 11 v 23), but was to be brought down to Hades for its rejection of the Saviour's ministry in that city. Guilty to a degree that is considered worse than Sodom and Gomorrah. A people whose very profession was to know and teach the scriptures.

17

Here was a man, brought by his friends or neighbours in a persevering manner, that the Saviour might heal him. Jesus's first words were most blessed "your sins are forgiven"; certain of the scribes reacted with the accusation of blasphemy, but the Saviour knew their thoughts and asks the question "which is the easier"? He then demonstrates His power saying to the palsied man "Arise, take up you bed and go home" and he arose and departed. There were at least five that day who believed the words of the Saviour, five, in scripture, being the number of grace with God, but weakness with men.

(ii)   The call of Matthew —— FORSAKING
Jesus in passing saw Matthew and said to him "Follow me". It was not Matthew that sought Jesus but Jesus sought Matthew. The publicans were always classed as sinners. It wound appear that the Lord went to the house of Matthew for a meal and many publicans and sinners were also present, much to the displeasure of the Pharisees who asked, "why does your master eat with publicans and sinners"?, addressed to the disciples, but Jesus heard and replied "They that are whole do not need a physician but they that are sick", "I came not to call the righteous but sinners ton repentance". The Lord was displaying God's grace and compassion (see Hosea ch. 6 v 6) and told them to go and learn.

(iii)   John's disciples and fasting —— FASTING
The bridegroom being present calls for joy and gladness, thus fasting was out of order. There was to be a new 'covenant' and a new order, where the law and ritual were to be displaced by grace and freedom 'If the Son shall make you free you shall be free indeed'. (see John ch. 8 v 36)

(iv) The woman who touched the hem of His garment.
      —— FAITH
      This was an intervention as the Lord travelled to the
      house of Jairus in which the Lord, despite the
      crowding of those that followed, was conscious of
      the touch of faith and asked his disciples "who
      touched me"? Having located the women in question
      the Lord gave the word of encouragement saying to
      her "your faith has healed you".

(v)   The   two   blind   men   and   the   mute.
      —— FORESIGHT
      The cry of the blind men gave indication of their
      concept of the person of the Lord insomuch as they
      cried "Son of David". The challenge of the Lord
      was "do you believe I am able to do this"?, their
      reply was "yes Lord" their faith was to yield their
      desire – they were made whole. The healing of the
      mute caused even more amazement, the people
      declaring "nothing liken this has ever been seen in
      Israel."

(vi) Where are the labourers? — —— FAITHFUL
      The chapter closes with the Lord challenging His
      disciples with regard to the need, after looking upon
      the large crowd, of labourers to reach out with the
      message of hope and salvation.

MATTHEW – CHAPTER 10

The call of the King

(1) His call of the disciples to Himself
(2) He gave them 'Authority'
(3) He sent them 'out'

The proclamation of the Kingdom of Heaven – verse 7

    (i) To the lost sheep of Israel – DIRECTION

    (ii) Take nothing with you – DEPENDENCE

    (iii) Seek some worthy person – DWELLING

    (iv) Preach peace and rest – DECLARATION

    (v) Be on your guard – DEFENCE

    (vi) You will be hated – DIVISIONS

    (vii) Do not be afraid – DELIBERATION

    (viii) Anyone who loves me – DEVOTION

They were to go proclaiming the 'Kingdom pf Heaven' is come
I am sending you out 'like sheep among wolves'
  You will be brought before governors and kings.

    (i) Exhortation

    (ii) Expectation

    (iii) Examination

MATTHEW – CHAPTER 11

(1)   Confirmation of the Coming of the King
(2)   Character of the voice proclaiming the King
(3)   Condemnation of the towns rejecting the King
(4)   Commendation of those receiving the King
  (i) Confirmation of the Coming of the King
       —— DETAIL
       (a) Are you 'the one' Details of birth seem
           forgotten
       (b) Tell John – What you have seen and heard
       (c) The blind receive sight, the good news is
           proclaimed etc. —— DECLARATION
       (d) Blessed are they who do not 'stumble'.
           —— DEDICATION
  (ii) Character of the voice proclaiming the King
       —— ENQUIRY
       What went you out to see?
       (a) A man dressed in finery —— EPECTATION
       (b) A prophet – more than a prophet ——
           EXCELLENCE
       (c) The great messenger – Elijah – the voice in
           the wilderness. —— ELIJAH
  (iii) Woes pronounced on – Chorazin, Bethsaida,
        Capernaaum, – cities highly privileged
  (iv) At that time!
       (a) Revealed to little children – INSTRUC TION
       (b) To know the Son – INTIMATION
       (c) Come to Me – Invitation —— INVITATION

21

MATTHEW – CHAPTER 12

(i)   The declaration of the King – verse 8

(ii)   The determination of the King – verse 12

(iii)   The directive of the King – verse 14

(iv)   The disapproval of the King – verse 32

(v)   The denial of the sign of the King – verse 39

(vi)   The direct relations of the King – verse 50

    (a) The Son of man — Lord of the Sabbath ——— PERSON
There were none to counter the claim

    (b) It was lawful to do good on the Sabbath ——— PRINCIPLES

    (c) Do not tell others – Let God speak ——— PROCLAMATION
(keep the word of scripture)

    (d) Every sin may be forgiven but not the sin of blasphemy against the Holy Spirit. (Not now nor in the age to come) —— PLEDGE

    (e) No sign to be given but that of Jonah – (Death & resurrection) —— PREDICTION

    (f) Direct relationship with Christ – Not physical but spiritual. ——— PLACE

MATTHEW – CHAPTER 13

The teachings of the King

(i) The parable of the Sower – Sowing the seed – v 3
our receptions to the seed sown; ——— SOWING
The path – rocks – thorns – soil
The path – birds of the air – open to all but
Impersonal.
Rocks – calloused – insensitive.
Thorns – choked by other influences.
Good soil – heard and embraced – fruit

(ii) Why speak in parables – SECRETS given – v 11
Those seeing they do not see and those hearing
they do not hear or understand

(iii) Fulfilment of Isaiah's prophecy – SCRIPTURES – v 14
The prophet Isaiah spoke of the hardness the nation
in rejecting their Messiah and His message (see
Isaiah chapter 6 verse 9)

(iv) Interpretation of Parable – SEEING & Hearing – v
18
The Lord explains the meaning of the parable to
His own, indicating each statement and its
interpretation so that they might understand.

(v) Parable of wheat & tares – SATAN'S work – v 24
The good seed is sown and sprouts, while everyone
sleeps the enemy comes and sows weeds. Upon
enquiry the master says "let both grow together"
ultimately he separates the wheat from the tares.

The weeds were destined to be burned and the Wheat to be gathered into the masters barns.

(vi) Parable of the mustard seed – Salvations SCOPE v31
The mustard seed is so very small but when planted grows into a tree to accommodate in its Branches. So the seed of the word of God when sown becomes so, accommodating both genuine as well as false
Parable of the Leaven – Social mixture —— SLUR
Leaven is always associated with evil in the scriptures, the present day church is contaminated with the evil leaven introduced over many years, where the spiritual has been demoted and the secular promoted.
Parable of weeds – The explanation of the ——
SEPARATION Parable of the tares, where the tares are the product of the evil one
Parables of treasure and pearls – Single sighted ——
SUBSTANCE

The treasure is the church as is the pearl of great price, the finder is the Lord himself who sold everything He had to purchase the treasure and the pearl.

The parable of the drag net. —— SALVATION
Gathered of every kind then
Sorted into good and bad. V's 47 – 50.

He came to His own town – began to teach
and was rejected.
Rejected not only his Teachings, but also His Person.

MATTHEW – CHAPTER 14

The authority of the King

(1) The folly of Herod – John beheaded – versus 1 –12

(2) The feeding of the five thousand – Loaves & fishes – verses 13 – 21

(3) The fearful storm – Walking on water – verses 22 – 33

(i) Fateful words spoken – the folly of Herod
—— FOOLISHNESS

> Oath made without forethought – a man void of conviction. when the flesh is 'elevated'

(ii) The pledge carried out – John beheaded

(iii) John's disciples took the body and buried it.

(2) The feeding of the five thousand.
—— FRUITFULNESS

(i) The disciples solution – 'Send them away'

(ii) The Lord's solution – They need not depart – You give them to eat

(iii) It is not a question of 'what we have'

(iv) But 'whom we have' – the Lord – the ALL SUFFICIENT one

(v) They all ate and were satisfied.

(3) The fearful storm —— FEARFULNESS

    (i)   Jesus made the disciples get into the boat

    (ii)   Jesus went up into the mountain to pray

    (iii)   The storm arose – the boat was buffeted by the waves

    (iv)   Jesus walks on the water

    (v)   Peter asks the Lord to 'bid him come'

    (vi)   Peter sinks – the Lord reaches out to 'Save him'

MATTHEW – CHAPTER 15

Features of the Kingdom

(1) The traditions of men – Hypocrites – verses 1 – 9
(2) The traits of the body – Defilement – verses 10 – 20
(3) The true faith – Even the dogs – versus 21 – 28
(4) The feeding of the 4000 – Have compassion – v's 32 – 39

  (i) The traditions of men, ——CUSTOM
    (a) You teach the people Human rules
      In the kingdom no traditions of men.
    (b) Out of the mouth comes defilement In the Kingdom nothing to defile.

  (ii) The traits of the body. —— CORRUPTION
    (a) They nullified the word of God
    (b) These people honour me with their lips but their hearts are far from me.

  (iii) The true faith —— CREDIT
    Taking the humble place is the key, the woman came
    and knelt before the Lord saying "Lord help me".
    The Lord answered "woman you have great faith Your request is granted".

  (v) The feeding of the 4000. —— COMPASSION
    (a) Jesus went up into the mountain and great crowds came to Him.

(b) Jesus called His disciples to Him saying "they have been with Me three days and have nothing to eat.

(c) "I do not want to send them away hungry"

(d) "How many loaves do you have" – "Seven" they reply." And a few small fish"

(e) Jesus told the crowd to sit down.

(f) He took the loaves and the fish, gave thanks, gave them to the disciples, who distributed to the crowd.

MATTHEW – CHAPTER 16

The king's warnings – confession – death

1. Seeking a sign.
2. The yeast of the Pharisees – Bread of softness – verses 5 – 16
3. The confession of Peter – You are the Christ – The Son of God – verses 17 – 20
4. Pronouncement of the Lord's death. – At the hands of religious leaders – verses 21 – 28

(1) Seeking a sign – Evil generation seeks a sign — EVIDENCE

   (i) You can read the signs in the sky

   (ii) You cannot interpret the signs of the times

   (iii) No sign given but the sign of the prophet Jonah.

(2) The yeast of the Pharisees – Bread of softness — ERROR

   (i) False teaching – re; the staff of life

   (ii) Beware of the leaven of the Pharisees and Sadducees

   (iii) Leaving out God's revelation o f His Son – who is the bread of lifeWho – means that the teaching of the Pharisees and Sadducees is of no effect.

(3) The confession of Peter – You are the Christ —— ENLIGHTENMENT

    (i) Who do the people say the Son of Man is?

    (ii) Some say John the Baptist, others Elijah, and even others Jeremiah.

    (iii) Whom do you say that I am?

    (iv) You are the Christ. – The Messiah – The Son of the Living God.

(4) Pronouncement of the Lord's death. —— ENIGMATIC

    (i) From that time Jesus explains to the disciples.

    (ii) Peter took him aside and said 'Never' – Lord replies 'Get you behind Me Satan –

    (iii) Satan has only human concerns – not the concerns of God

    (iv) Those who will follow Jesus must lose their life to be able to find it.

MATTHEW – CHAPTER 17

The king – His glory – the witness of His power – His death

1. The transfiguration of Jesus – Moses and Elijah – verses 1 – 9
2. The question regarding Elijah – John the Baptist – verse 10 – 13
3. The demon possessed boy – The disciples failure – verses 14 – 21
4. Jesus predicts His death – In Galilee – verses 22 – 23
5. The temple tax – The coin in the fishes mouth – verses 24

(1) The transfiguration of Jesus ––––– TRANSFIGURATION

    (i) Peter, James& John – the mountain top experience – verses 1 – 9

    (ii) The presence of Moses and Elijah. – The law & the Prophets – verses 10 – 13

    (iii) The voice from heaven – this is My Beloved Son – The person

    (iv) In whom I am well pleased – The Pleasure

    (v) Hear ye Him – the Proclaimer

(2) The question regarding Elijah. ––––– TEACHING

    (i) I tell you Elijah has already come. – they did not recognise him

(ii) The disciples understood that He spoke of John the Baptist

(3) The demon possessed boy —— TERROR

    (i) A man approached – Lord have mercy on my son

    (ii) Bring the boy to Me – Jesus rebuked the demon

    (iii) The disciples – Why couldn't we drive it out?

    (iv) Because you have so little faith.

    (v) This kind does not go out except by prayer and fasting.

(4) Jesus predicts His death. – In Galilee —— TREACHERY

    (i) In Galilee Jesus said to them the Son of Man will be killed'

    (ii) The disciples were filled with grief.

(5) The temple tax – does your teacher pay the temple tax? —— TAXATION

    (i) In the house the Lord asks Peter 'of whom do the kings of the earth collect tax.

    (ii) From others answered Peter.

    (iii) So that we may not cause offence

    (iv) Go thrown out your line – first fish caught open its mouth find a coin use that to pay.

MATTHEW – CHAPTER 18

The kingdom – Place – People – Personal relations

(1) Who is greatest in the Kingdom – A child – v's 1 – 3
(2) Stumbling a 'little child ' – Hinderances – v's 4 – 14
(3) Parable of the Lost sheep – Seeking the Lost – v's 15 – 19
(4) Dealing with sin in the church – Discipline – v's 20 – 26
(5) A lesson in forgiveness – The evil servant – v's 27 – 35

    (i)   Who is the greatest in the Kingdom? – A child
        – STATUS
        Childlike characteristics, whoever takes the lowly position of a child will be greatest in the Kingdom of Heaven.

    (ii) Avoid causing stumbling. —— STUMBLING
        The judgements on those who cause such little ones to stumble are quite uncompromising; it is better to take radical action to avoid such a thing happening than to commit such an act that that may mean failure to enter life and end up in the fire of hell.

    (iii) Parable of the lost sheep. —— SEEKING
        The Son of Man came to seek and to save that which was lost. The finding of the lost sheep is a cause for great rejoicing in heaven; it is the will of the Father that none of these little ones perish.

    (iv) Sin and its discipline —— SAFEGUARDING
        Sin in the church between individuals is to be dealt with in the way set out. If there is a refusal to accept then let the church deal with the matter, if there is

further refusal, treat them as the pagan. Agreement between two is to be commended and blessed by the Father and where two or three are gathered in 'my name' there am I in the midst of them.

(v) A lesson in forgiveness ——— SET FREE
The question of Peter was an opportunity to illustrate the forgiveness of |God. |The king in the parable was rightfully acting when he first pronounced his judgement but on the pleading of the servant took pity on him and cancelled the debt. That same servant did the opposite to his fellow servant and thus, when the king was told, he exercised his authority to judge the servant, so will the Father do unless you forgive your brother or sister from your heart.

MATTHEW – CHAPTER 19

The king rules and directs

1. The question of divorce – What the law required – verse 1 – 12
2. The Lord and the children – Suffer them to come to Me
3. The rich and the kingdom of God.

   (1) The question of divorce —— HARDNESS

      (i)   Is it lawful for a man to divorce his wife

      (ii) It was not so from the beginning – haven't you read

      (iii) What God has joined let no man put asunder.

      (iv) Why did Moses write a man may give his wife a certificate.

      (v)   Because of the hardness of your hearts

      (vi) It is better not to marry – some are born eunuchs, others made of men.

   (2) The Lord and the children. —— HINDERANCE

      (i)   Let the little come to Me.

      (ii) Do not hinder them – the kingdom of heaven belongs to such as these.

      (iii) He laid His hands on them.

(3) The rich and the kingdom of God. —— HEAVINESS

    (i) Good master – What shall I do?

    (ii) Keep the commandments.

    (iii) All these have I kept from my youth up.

    (iv) One thing you lack – sell all that you have and give to the poor

    (v) He went away sad for he had great wealth.

    (vi) Jesus said " It is hard for someone who has riches tp enter the Kingdom of God.

    (vii) The disciples then asked "Who then can be saved"

    (viii) The things that are impossible with men are possible with God.

MATTHEW – CHAPTER 20

The king – His words and His will

1. The parable of the workers. – 1st Last and last 1st. – verses 1 – 16
2. Jesus predicts His death – This is the third occasion. – 17 – 19
3. Mother of John and James – Request for place in the kingdom. – verses 0 – 28
4. Two blind men – healed – verses 29 – 34

(1) Parable of the workers —— REWARD

   (i) Denarius – for the day's work.

   (ii) Denarius – for part of the day's work.

   (iii) Lesson – Master decides – His resources outgoing

(2) Jesus predicts His death. —— REJECTION

   (i) This is then third time He has done so.

   (ii) Three times recorded by Matthew

   (iii) The Son of Man will be delivered.

(3) The request of the mother of John and James was met with the words of the — REQUEST
Saviour "you do not know what you are asking".
This was something that was in the Father's hands.

(4) It is significant that the miracle following is the healing of two blind men. Blindness is a complaint that restricts vision, such was the lesson of the previous request, where

(5) the vision was misplaced as indicated by the Lord.
—— REVELATION

MATTHEW – CHAPTER 21

The Kings reception, the King in his temple, the Kings curse, the Kings authority, the Kings will, the Kings servants.

(1) Entry of Jesus as King – Jerusalem – Verse 1 – 11
(2) Jesus in the temple – Overturns tables – verses 12 – 17
(3) Jesus curses the fig tree – Faiths power – verses 18 – 22
(4) Authority of Jesus questioned – Challenge – verses 23 – 27
(5) Parable of two sons – Promises – verse 28 – 33
(6) Parable of the Tenants – Stone rejected – verses 34 – 44

   (i)   Entry of the King – Hosanna ——— PRAISE
       The fulfilment of scripture is here evidence of His Kingship testified by the cry of the crowd raising to the highest heaven.

   (ii) Jesus in the Temple – Tables overthrown —— PERVERSION
       This was followed by entry to the temple. How different from entry to the city. The trading condemned, the tables being overturned and the declaration concerning the Father's house.

   (iii) Curse of the Fig tree – No fruit —— PRETENCE
       The search for fruit by the Saviour and it being absent caused the speaking of the curse, the Fig tree being a symbol of Israel nationally and lacking fruit.

   (iv) Jesus's authority – Baptism of John —— PESSIMISM

The chief priests and the elders challenged the authority of the Lord and who gave Him that authority. Jesus then asked one question 'the baptism of John, where did it come from'? Upon being given an answer Jesus promised to tell them the answer to their question. They failed to answer and said we do not know thus Jesus said "Neither do I tell you by what authority I do these things."

(v)   The parable of the two sons. —— PROMISES

A lesson in repentance is the focus of this parable where the one son said 'no' at first and then repented, whilst the second son said yes and did not go. The application of the parable the Lord makes known in relation to the preaching of John the Baptist.

(vi)   Parable   of   tenants   –   Responsibility
—— POSSESSION

This parable reinforces the lessons of the previous parable but with much more serious implications as it is the Son of God speaking and the treatment He received as a result of His ministry 'the stone which the builders rejected', but God made Him the cornerstone.

MATTHEW – CHAPTER 22

He King sets out the requirements of kingdom

(1) The king's wedding banquet – Invitations rejected – v's 1 – 14

(2) Paying poll tax to Caesar – Is it right – verses 15 – 22

(3) Marriage after the resurrection – No marriage – verses 23 –34

(4) The greatest commandment – Love God – verses 35 – 40

(5) Whose Son is Messiah – David's Son – verses 41 – 45

    (i)   The banquet; —— INVITATION
        (a)   Invitation refused
        (b)   Servants killed
        (c)   Streets and highways searched
        (d)   Individual without garment

    (ii) Give to Caesar what is His – and give to God what is His

The Pharisees once again plan for the trapping of the Lord in His words, but the Lord was aware of their intent and asked for the coin of the realm and posed the question whose superscription is this, then when the answer came so also the challenge 'Give to Caesar what is his and to God what is His. – INSTRUCTION

    (iii) Marriage – like the angels in heaven —— INDICATION

Here they were in error not knowing the scriptures but relying on their own reasoning. How dangerous!!

(iv)   The commandment – Love – God and neighbour – IRRECVOCABLE
Love never fails (see 1Corinthians 13 verse 8.)

(v)   Whose Son is Messiah – INQUIRY
How does David address Him so?
"The Lord said unto MY LORD"
Messiah was David's Lord

MATTHEW – CHAPTER 23

The king's judgement

1. A warning against hypocrisy – verses 1 – 12
2. Seven woes pronounced – verses 13 – 36
3. Appeal to Jerusalem – verses 37 – 39
    (1) A warning against hypocrisy – verses 1– 12 – Seeking notoriety by outward show
       (i) They do nothing without people observing them —— WARNINGS
       (ii) They do not practice what they preach
       (iii) They love the honour at banquets3
       (iv) They love to be greeted with respect in the market places
       (v) They love to be called 'Rabbi' by others

    (2) Seven woes pronounced ——— WOES
       (i) Woe unto you Pharisees and teachers of the la
       (ii) Youn shut the door of the Kingdom of heaven in peoples faces
       (iii) Youn recruit from abroad a single soul and make them twice a child of hell
       (iv) Woe to you blind guides
       (v) Woe to you hypocrites – you 'have neglected justice, mercy and faithfulness.

(vi) Woe to you hypocrites – you strain at a gnat and swallow a camel

(vii) Woe to you hypocrites – you clean the outside but inside full of greed & indulgence.

(3) Appeal to Jerusalem ——— WEEPING

    (i) Jerusalem Jerusalem how I have longed to gather your children together

    (ii) You were not willing

    (iii) Your house is left to you desolate

    (iv) You will not see me again until you say ———

MATTHEW – CHAPTER 24

The King's predictions – Time and Hour

(1) Destruction of the Temple – Sign of the end times – v's
(2) The day and the Hour unknown

    (i)   As to the destruction – Sign – Future – SIGNS
The disciples asked "what shall be the sign of your coming"? "When shall this happen"? The destruction of the temple came in AD 70 but the Lord indicated those things that must take place before the coming of the Son of Man such as false claims of Messiahship, wars and rumours of wars, increase of wickedness, the abomination of desolation in the temple, distress among the nations, sun, moon and stars and heavenly bodies shaken. Then will appear the Sign of the Son of Man.

    (ii)   The Day and the Hour – Unknown – SCENES
The Saviour makes known that the actual day and hour has not been revealed and only the Father knows of that time. There are incidents referred to, which will take place at that moment of revelation, where division between those that are ready and those not so.

MATTHEW – CHAPTER 25

The King's Revelations

(1) The Parable of the Ten Virgins – Wise/ foolish v's 1 – 13
(2) Parables of the Bags of Gold – Well Done – v's 14 – 32
(3) Parable of Sheep and Goats – Come/ Depart v's 33 – 46

   (i) Parable of the ten virgins – Preparedness – READINESS
       (a) Wise – prepared – Oil in Jars
       (b) Foolish – unprepared – no oil

   (ii) Parable of the Gold – Posterity — REQIREMENT
       (a) Bags allocated
       (b) Master leaves
       (c) Servants invest – all but one
       (d) Master returns
       (e) Judgement exercised

   (iii) Sheep and Goats – Prospect — REALISATION
       (a) Congregate
       (b) Separated
       (c) Placed accordingly

MATTHEW – CHAPTER 26

The king's popularity – Hailed – worshipped – betrayed – judged – mocked – denied

(1) Plot against Jesus ———— DEPRAVITY

    (i) Chief priests and elders – religious leaders – persuaded the people – verses 1–7

    (ii) Out of hate and envy – because the Lord condemned them

(2) Jesus anointed at Bethany – Mary – verses 8 – 13 ——— DEVOTION

    (i) Mary pours precious ointment over the Lord

    (ii) Mary condemned / commended – the Lord recognises her perception

(3) Judas agrees to betray Jesus – for a sum of money – verses 14 – 16 —— DECEIT

    (i) Iscariot induced by money – 30 pieces

    (ii) Plan contrived – betrayed by a kiss

    (iii) Ultimately regretted his act – hanged himself

(4) The last supper – With His disciples – Last time with His own – verses 17 – 34 —— DESIRE

    (i) With desire did the Lord anticipate this gathering

    (ii) The last time before His death

(iii) The denial by Peter revealed

(iv) The Gethsemane experience – disciples asleep – Saviour's agony

(v) Here comes my betrayer

(5) Jesus Arrested – a large crowd with Judas – verses 41 – 45 —— DEMONIC

   (i) Where his loyalty lay?

   (ii) His act of false devotion in the kiss

   (iii) Do what you came for friend said Jesus

(6) Jesus before Sanhedrin – Biassed judges – verses 46 – 51 —— DEVIOUSNESS

   (i) An unfair trial

   (ii) False witnesses

(7) Peter disowns Jesus – Fear of Man – verses 52 – 64 —— DENIAL

   (i) Peter confronted by various ones

   (ii) Peter decides to disown his association with Jesus

   (iii) Peter goes out and weeps.

MATTHEW – CHAPTER 27

The King's Sufferings

(1) Judas hangs himself – Regret – verses 1 – 10
(2) Jesus before Pilate – Relents – verses 11 –26
(3) Jesus crucified – Rejection – verses 27 – 34
(4) Jesus and the thieves – Realisation – verses 35 – 44
(5) Jesus's Death – Release – verses 45 – 52
(6) Jesus in the tomb – Reassurance – verses 53 – 57

(i) Judas's death – Regret
What an end for one who had the privilege of being with the Lord for those three or more years, to hear His teachings and witness His miracles yet not entering into His gift of Salvation.

(ii) Jesus/Pilate – Relents
Another individual who was privileged to hear the words of the Saviour but chose to listen to the cry of the crowd and to hand over the Saviour to their will.

(iii) Jesus crucified – Rejection
The rejection of the Lord by His own people with the words "His blood be upon us and our chidren" was to be paid in full by the future that the nation suffered under the judgement of God.

(iv) Jesus and the thieves – Realisation

In the midst of indescribable suffering the Saviour found words of hope for the repentant thief, manifesting such mercy and grace.

(v) Jesus's Death – Release
The moment of the death of was Jesus was marked with certain events, the cry Eli Eli Lema Sabaccthani. a further cry uttered and Jesus gave up His spirit, at that moment the curtain of the temple was torn in two from top to bottom, the earth shook and the rocks split.

(vi) Of Jesus in the tomb – Reassurance
Because of the words of Jesus the chief priests and the elders went to Pilate to ask action to vouchsafe the dead body. A guard was provided and a seal placed on the tomb until the third day, but in vain because on the third day He arose.

MATTHEW – CHAPTER 28

The King's victory

(i) Resurrection glory – God's vindication – REJOICING
The resurrection is the irrefutable proof of the Kingship of the Son of God and the vindication of God's plan of redemption. He is not here, he has risen were the words of the angel to the women at the tomb.

(ii) Report connived – His body was stolen —— REINSTATE
Some of the guards went into the city and reported to the chief priests 'everything that had happened'. The chief priests with the elders concocted a plan, giving the guards a large sum of money to say His disciples came and stole the body, this story being widely circulated.

(iii) Re – commission – Go into all the world —— RECOMMENDATION
(i) Not only Israel
(ii) But all the Gentiles
(iii) Preach the good news

OUTLINES IN THE GOSPEL OF MARK

The second gospel has for its design, the setting forth of the service "of Jesus Christ, the Son of God"

(W. Kelly – Exposition of the Gospel of Mark – Paternoster – London)

MARK – CHAPTER 1

The chapter gives details of what the Son of God came to earth for. That is, to manifest His person and declare, by works, the gospel of the grace of God to all mankind.

Divisions of the chapter:

An amazing beginning – verses 1 – 8
An essential baptism – verses 9 – 13
A purposeful bidding – verses 17 – 22
A powerful boldness – verses 23 – 28
An appointed bond – verses 29 – 39
An applied blessing – verses 40 – 45

An Amazing Beginning – verses 1 – 8

W Barcley says "It began long, long ago in the mind of God".

Jesus Christ – the Son of God – The Person who is the Beginning – v 1.

As it is written – so it stands – The Prophets who proclaimed it – v 2

There comes One more mighty – The Promise fulfilled by God – v 7

An Essential Baptism – verses 9 –13.

"The Moment of 'Identification'", W Barcley

Jesus came. was baptised – The Place – Jordan verse 9

Coming up out of the water – The Presence – the Spirit like a dove – v 10

The voice speaking – The Pronouncement – My Beloved Son – v 11

A Purposeful Bidding – verses 14 – 22

"It was no question of the law but of repentance", W Kelly.

Jesus came into Galilee – Preaching the gospel – Repent and believe – v15

Purpose, fulfilling God's plan – Predetermined – Time is fulfilled – v15

Come after me – The Plea – become my disciples – v17

A Powerful Boldness – verses 23 – 28

"The Lord would receive no testimony from demons". J Heading

I know you who you are ——————Perception – the Holy one of God – v 24

He came out of him ——————Power – could not disobey – ———v 27

His fame spread ----------------------- Prominence – standing out ———v 28

An Appointed Bond – verses 29 – 39

"The human tones of the mind of Christ are vivid here" J G. Bellet.

A response to need – Personal empathy – verse 30

Finding the solitary place – Prayer – He went out – verse 35

All men seek you – Popularity – Let us go – verse 38

Why I came forth – Preaching – And He preached – verse 39

An Applied Blessing – verses 40 – 45

"'Moved with compassion', Mark alone describes the Saviour's feelings", J Alexander

If you will, you can –	Preconception	verse 40
Jesus said 'I will' –	Predisposition	verse 41
He was cleansed –	Product	verse 42
A work for a testimony –	Proof	verse 44
He went out and began –	Publishing	verse 45

CHAPTER 1 –
POINTS TO NOTE

1. Marks emphasis is on the servant character 'of the Lord Jesus, hence he begins his gospel with the prophet declaration from Isaiah 'Behold I send my messenger —— the voice of one crying in the wilderness 'Prepare the way of the Lord', make straight His Paths – there comes one mightier than I, after me, He shall baptize you with the Holy Ghost.

2. Mark is the only gospel writer who tells us, that in the forty days of temptation, 'He was with the wild beasts', who were submissive to him at the beginning of His ministry. Sadly, at the end of His ministry 'human beasts' heaped their hatred upon Him (see Mark Ch. 15).

3. As God's servant His acts, miracles, words etc, created an impact of immediacy as is indicated by the record in this chapter (note the occurrence of the words – straightway, immediately, as soon as He had spoken etc.

4. Whilst Matthew records the event (i. e. the cleansing of the leper and what followed and closes with the Lord's command to tell no one), Mark goes further and indicates the man going out to proclaim the fact of his cure and to circulate the words of the Saviour.

MARK – CHAPTER 2

This chapter deals with the issues of Forgiveness, Following, Favour, Fasting and Freedom. These are presented by the Lord himself to the Pharisees, the Scribes and the Publicans.

Divisions of the chapter:

A lesson on forgiveness   verses 1– 12
A word to follow and Divine favour   verses 13 – 17
A directive on fasting and freedom   verses 18 – 28

A lesson on Forgiveness – verses 1 – 12

"The Saviour acts in the sovereignty of grace" W Barcley

He preached the word – What He spoke.   verse 2
He saw their faith   – What He saw.   verse 5
He said "son, your sins are forgiven" – What He said.
verse 5
He challenged them   – What He reasoned. verse 9
They were all amazed – What He wrought. verse 12

A Word to follow – verses 13 – 17
"It was an essential of the Jewish faith that 'only God can forgive sins'. " – W Barcley

As He passed by   – What He saw – verse 14
The personal call   – What He spoke – verse 14
The immediate response – What He effected – verse 14

The words of the Pharisees & scribes – What He heard – verse 17
How He responded – What He declared – verse 17
Why He came – What He purposed – verse 17

A directive on fasting and freedom verses 18 –28 – Quote: Man came first and the sabbath after – J. Heading
The question posed – What He answered – verse 19
The bridegrooms presence – What He revealed – verse 19
The bridegrooms parting – What He anticipated – verse 20
The lesson that followed – What He taught – verse 21 & 22 – New cloth and new wine
The breaking of the Sabbath – What He answered – verse 24 – Plucking ears of corn
The Sabbath and its place – What He declared – verse 27 – Made for man
The Lord of the Sabbath – What He claimed – verse 28 – The Son of Man

CHAPTER 2 –
POINTS TO NOTE

1. Matthew's account of the healing of the paralytic is brief (see Matthew ch. 9 v's 1–8) Mark & Luke are more detailed. Mark tells us they let down the bed, whilst Luke tells us he was brought in a bed, obviously the man was helpless as to mobility. The sinner is helpless to move towards God, it is the Holy Spirit that takes the initiative.

2. All three gospel records list the accusation to the Lord of' speaking blasphemies'. Thus the Lord addressed them with the challenge "why reason ye (think you evil) in your hearts".

3. The accusation of the Pharisees re; eating and drinking with publicans and sinners, was repelled by the Lord, as the three writers of the gospels record the words of the Lord "I came not to call the righteous but sinners to 'repentance'. the righteous referred to are those who claim absolute righteousness thus exempting all humankind".

MARK – CHAPTER 3

This chapter brings to our attention the exercise of Divine Power in various situations ie. Healing on the sabbath day, the ordaining of the chosen twelve, declaration of the end of Satan and his followers.

Divisions of the chapter:

A manifestation of Divine grief – verses 1 – 7
A witness to Divine power – verses 8 – 12
A dispensing of Divine favour – verses 13 – 19
A declaration of Divine import – verses 20 – 35

A manifestation of Divine grief verses 1 – 7 Quote: He manifested grief as a man – acquainted with grief – J. Heading
They watched Him – a critical scrutiny – verse 2 – whether He would heal
The Saviour's command – a command of authority – verse 3 – He said to the 'man' – personal address
The question asked – a challenge to answer – verse 4 – Is it lawful? – they held their peace
Straightway – a counsel to kill – verse 6 – How they might destroy

A witness to Divine Power verses 8 – 12 – Quote: 'having heard how many great things He was doing' – J. A. Alexander
When they heard – a word that spread – verse 8 – a great multitude followed Him
They pressed upon him – a wish to be healed – verse 9 – lest they should throng Him

Unclean spirits cried – a witness refused – verse 12 – He straightly charged them
to initiate a way of disseminating His message – W. Barcley
He ordained twelve – Divine authority – verse 14 – that He might send them forth to preach
To have power – Divine delegation – verse 15 – to work miracles of healing
Even Judas – Divine foreknowledge – verse 15 – and Judas Iscariot which also betrayed Him – verse 19

A Declaration of Divine Import verses 20 – 35 – Quote: if Satan rises up against himself – he cannot subsist – he has an end – W. Kelly

CHAPTER 3 –
POINTS TO NOTE

1. Healing on the sabbath day was forbidden by the religious leaders of the day (see Luke ch. 13 v 14), but grace was to replace 'Law', there was now 'new wine' which could not be housed in 'old bottles'.

2. It is noteworthy that the company called the 'twelve' were a mixture of individuals of different backgrounds and occupations eg. Matthew – the tax collector, Simon – the Canaanite (zealot), Peter, James & John – fishermen, Judas – possibly the Lord's brother, all of which had different opinions, but all forming a company in union with and following after the Lord.

3. The attributes of miraculous working was, by the scribes, stated as being by Beelzebub, the prince of devils, but Mark chapter 3 verse 11 indicates that the unclean spirits fell down before Him saying, 'Thou art the Son of God'.

MARK – CHAPTER 4

This chapter brings before us the fact that the Son of God extends His teaching to a wider audience in the open air, but in parabolic form so that the Spirit of God can work in hearts of the hearers, to bring about an understanding of the word spoken. The Lord uses everyday activities, easily recognised and identified with to illustrate the mysteries of the kingdom of God and its entry.

THE LORD'S DOCTRINE – verses 1–9–Quote: He was ready and willing to take preaching and teaching out of its conventional setting into the open air – W Barcley
He taught many things – verse 2– Parabolic instruction
A parable of importance – verse 3 Plea to listen – hearken
He that has ears to hear – verse 9 Personal challenge

THE LORD'S DECLARATION – VERSE 10 – 23–Quote: The mystery here particularly means 'the kingdom of God – J. A. Alexander'

Understanding God's word – verse 12 – Prophetic prediction (see Isaiah chapter 6 verse 9 & 10)

Revelation given – verse 14 – Practical application – The Sower sows the word

If any have ears to hear – verse 23 – Plain explanation – Nothing hidden (verse 22).

The Lord's deliberation – verses 24 – 34 – Quote: We have the responsibility to shine in the world, holding forth the word of life. – W. Kelly

Take heed what you hear – verse 24 – A warning to watch – what measure you mete
Do not sleep – verse 27 – A Wakeful spirit – when the fruit is brought forth
To what do we liken the 'kingdom of God' – A Wise comparison – when it is sown it grows

The Lord's demonstration – verse 35 – 41 – Quote: If the Son does not sink neither shall we – J. N. Darby
A great storm – verse 37 – A full ship – Not with people but with waves of water
A great fear – verse 38 – A fear of death – carest thou not that we perish?
A great calm – verse 39 – A faith that delivers – why are you so fearful?
A great amazement – verse 41 – A frank discovery – what manner of man is this?

CHAPTER 4 –
POINTS TO NOTE

1. In the four cases stated Mark gives a brief account of the fate of the seed sown as does Matthew, but Luke tells us more eg. the seed was trodden down (see Luke ch. 8 v 5). In the second case the seed had no moisture, in the third instance the thorns grew with the seed and in the fourth the seed grew.

2. The call to 'hear' is issued and recorded by each gospel account. Also is the statement 'to you it is given to know', no blindness involved, but for the rest (religious leaders) blindness continues, ie seeing they see not and hearing they hear not. But blessed are they (the disciples) added by Matthew in his account.

3. Verse 26 introduces another parable peculiar to Mark's gospel, 'So is the kingdom of God' with no warning as to what they heard and how they proceeded (see Matthew ch. 13) in light of the coming harvest.

4. The occasion of the storm is one that Mark, in his account, focusses on the time of the incident ie. 'it was when evening was come', whereas Luke states 'on a certain day'. The experience of the storm was to be a spiritual lesson to demonstrate the power of the Saviour when the storms of life come, He is not unaware, but is in control to secure a safe outcome and restore calm to the situation.

MARK – CHAPTER 5

The chapter records for us the details of three major encounters in the ministry of the Lord Jesus and the miracles that followed each having different circumstances, and each being uniquely met with his compassion and power
to effect deliverance from the effects of the sin of Adam passed on to the human race.

A recognition of Jesus as the Son of the Most high God – verses 1 – 10
A revelation of the authority of Jesus over demons – verses 11 – 13
A request to depart – verses 14 – 17
A ruler's plea – verses 20 – 23
A reason to confess – verses 24 – 34
A reliable word – verses 35 – 43

A recognition of Jesus as the Holy one of God – verses 1 – 10 – Quote: What have I to do with you? – Literally what have we in common? – J. Heading
He ran and worshipped Him – verse 6 – A vain worship – The Lord would not receive such from demons
A request for no further torment – verse 7 – A vocal request – The demons actually speak
The unclean spirits went out – verse 13 – A violent end – They choked in the sea

A revelation of the authority of Jesus over demons – verses 11 – 13 – Quote: He immediately permitted them (ie. He gave them leave) – J. A. Alexander

My name is Legion for we are many – verse 9 – A Plurality of possession – change from I to we

All the devils besought Him – verse 12 – A petition requested – Send us

Forthwith Jesus gave them leave – verse 13 – A permission granted

A request to depart – verses 14 – 17 – Quote: The man felt that the demons were asking not to be totally destroyed – W. Barcley

The unclean spirits went out – verse 13 – An obedience unopposed

They ran violently – verse 14 – An open witness

Choked in the sea – verse 15 – An outcome due

A ruler's plea – verses 20 – 24 – Quote: The man showed faith in the Lord's healing power – J. Heading

Besought Him greatly – verse 23 – An urgent matter – this required urgent attention

My little daughter – verse 23 – An unquiet approach – the father was in real distress

At the point of death – verse 23 – An ultimate end – the brink of lifes end

Jesus went with him – verse 24 – An unquestioned empathy – despite the throng

A reason to confess – verses 25 – 34 – Quote: Many have come to Jesus Christ when at their wits end – W. Barcley

A certain woman – verse 25 – An unnamed person – Jesus deals with the whosoever comes to Him

An issue of blood – verse 25 – An unremitting disease – spent all seeking a cure

Nothing bettered – verse 26 – An unsuccessful search – after many attempts

If I may but touch His clothes – verse 27 – An unbelievable faith – uninvited but confident.

Jesus immediately knowing – verse 30 – An unreasonable question – Who touched Me?

The woman came and confessed to him – verse 33 – An unbidden confession – Told Him all the truth

A reliable word – verses 35 – 43 – Quote: Do not regard the child as dead but think of her as asleep – J. A. Alexander

They laughed Him to scorn – verse 40 – A carnal response – such is man's thinking

He takes the father and the mother – verse 40 – A comforting act – the Saviour's empathy

He took the damsel by the hand – verse 41 – An close attraction – the love of Jesus

Talitha cumi – Damsel arise verse 41 – A commanding word – the authority of Christ over death

They were astonished – verse 42 – A conclusive end – removing all doubt

CHAPTER 5 –
POINTS TO NOTE

1. This chapter contains the accounts of various miracles illustrating distinct examples of the power of the Saviour claimed and exercised, ie. power over demons, healing where man had failed to cure, and thirdly power over death in the restoring of the damsel.

2. The request to depart was based on the fear 'they were afraid and the loss (only Mark records) and also concerning the swine. The secular and material was considered more important than the welfare of the demon possessed man and his healing.

3. The healing of the woman with the issue of blood and Jairus's daughter are reordered by all the gospel writers but it is Mark who seems to focus in greater detail and tells us that the situation grew worse (ch. 5 v 6). The action of the woman seemed to be the 'last resort'. As regards Jairus's daughter all Three gospel writers record 'the damsel is not dead but sleeps', but Luke adds 'knowing that she was dead' (ch. 8 v 53).

MARK – CHAPTER 6

This chapter contains information of events which are truly mixed in terms of outcome eg. The rejection of Jesus by his own country, the calling and commission of the twelve, the despicable decision of Herod, the feeding of the 5000 and the calming of the storm.

Divisions of the chapter:

V's 1 –6 A prophet without honour
V's 7 –13 A preaching of repentance
V's14 – 29 A pernicious act
V's 30 – 44 A Phenomenal miracle
V's 45 – 56 A Particular revelation

V's 1 – 6 A prophet without honour

- (i) Came to His own country – The place v 1
- (ii) He began to teach – The purpose v 2
- (iii) Could not do a mighty work – The prejudice v 3
- (iv) He marvelled – The personal reaction v 6

V's 7 – 13 A preaching of repentance

- (i) The commission to preach – Authority v 7
- (ii) The command to go in Faith – Application v 8
- (iii) The condemnation of rejection – Appraisal v 11
- (iv) The Complete obedience – Accord v 12

V's 14 – 29 A pernicious act.

   (i)   A false deduction – Assumption v 14

   (ii)   A fear of John – Affectation v 20

   (iii)   A foolish offer – Appeasement v 22

   (iv)   A Frightful request – Advice v 25

   (v)   A Fateful outcome – Action v 27

V's 30 – 44 A phenomenal miracle

   (i)   A place of rest – No leisure v 31

   (ii)   A people without a shepherd – No Leader v 34

   (iii)   A problem without a solution – No leeway v 37

   (iv)   A provision more than enough – No Lack v's 42/43

   (v)   A private prayer time – No laxity v 46

V's 45 – 56 A particular revelation

   (i)   Separated physically – Spiritual separation v 47

   (ii)   Seeing things differently – Seeing is believing v's 48/49

   (iii)   Speaking encouragement – Saviour's succour v 50

   (iv)   Sudden recognition – Sight restored v 54

   (v)   Saving touch – Saviour's presence v 56

CHAPTER 6 –
POINTS TO NOTE

1. Mark, in his gospel, gives some detail of the reception received by the Lord in His own country. The people registered his upbringing, his family ties, his occupation etc but not his teaching. "Whence has this man these tings having never learned" – and they were offended at Him. This was possibly the first visit, of two recorded, (see Luke ch. 4 verses 15–30).
2. No mighty works could be wrought among them; Luke, in his account, goes further and declares details of their rejection of the Saviour, so that in the synagogue, all were filled with wrath (anger).
3. The taking of the Lord, by the people, and their desire to destroy Him, is not recorded by Mark, but it is by Luke. Luke does not record the healing of the few sick by the Saviour as does Mark.

MARK – CHAPTER 7

The beginning of this chapter deals with defilement and its source, followed by the Syrophoenician woman's plea and the Saviour's response and the healing of the deaf man.

Main divisions of the chapter:

V's 1 – 23 – Defilement and its source
V's 24 – 30 – Determination and its reward
V's 31 – 37 – Deafness and its removal

V's 1 – 23 Defilement and its source

   (i)   Tradition and the commandments – verses 6 – 8

  (ii)   Trampling on the Word of God – verses 9 – 13

 (iii)   Teaching the Truth – verses 14 – 16

V's 24 – m 30 Determination and its reward

   (i)   A gentile woman – Syrophoenician woman v 26

  (ii)   A Generous spirit – Submission v 28

 (iii)   A great faith – Salvation sought v 28

 (iv)   A Gracious Savour – Salvation gained v 29

  (v)   A good outcome – Sadness into Joy v 30

V's 31 – 37 Deafness removed

   (i)   Brought one that was deaf – Beseeching v 32

  (ii)   Be opened – Blessing v 33

 (iii)   Beyond measure – Boundless v 37

CHAPTER 7 –
POINTS TO NOTE

1. Mark gives more detail than Matthew in relation to this event of the Pharisees accusing the disciples and the Saviour of neglect of tradition in regard to hygiene and the necessity of washing before engaging in eating. The Saviour calls them 'hypocrites' for replacing the commandments of God with the traditions of men.
2. Both Mark and Matthew record the words of the Lord in response to the accusation of the Pharisees saying, "You make the Word of God of none effect" Such is the heart and actions of man to set the Word of God as lacking in requirement and not sufficient to meet his need.
3. The important lesson to be learned is that of which the Saviour declared "Defilement comes from within and not from without; it is that which comes from within that defiles a man".

MARK – CHAPTER 8

This chapter records the miracle of the feeding of the four thousand and later confirms

The two miracles of the feeding of the five thousand and the four thousand. It also gives warning of the leaven of the Pharisees, records the healing of the blind man and the confession of the disciple of the Lord and His identity.

The main divisions of the chapter:

V's 1 – 9 – Satisfaction of the hungry.
V's 10 – 21 – Signs and Leaven
V's 22 – 26 – Sight restored
V's 27 – 38 – Spirit given revelation

V's 1– 9 Satisfaction of the hungry

(i) Nothing to eat – Seeing the Need v's 1 & 2

(ii) Not able to provide – Source not available v 5 (wilderness)

(iii) Nothing wasted – Sufficient and more v 8 (7 Baskets)

V's 10 – 21 – Signs and Leaven

(i) Why seek a sign? – Wrong motives – verse 11

(ii) Why do you not understand? – Wrong reasoning – verse 16

(iii) Why do you not see? – Wrong perception – verse 17

V's 22 – 26 – Sight restored

    (i)   Blind man brought – Desiring His touch verse 22

    (ii)   Blessed hands – Divine touch – verse 22 & 25 (Hands)

    (iii)   Blessing bestowed – Definite healing – verse 25 9 Saw clearly

V's 27 – 38 Spirit given revelation

    (i)   The challenge issued – Opinions given – verses 27 & 28

    (ii)   The confession spoken – Outspoken Peter

    (iii)   The charge given – Oncoming rejection

    (iv)   The rebuke of Peter – Objection rebuffed

    (v)   The preciousness of the Soul – Overiding purpose

CHAPTER 8 –
POINTS TO NOTE

1. The feeding of the four thousand presented two major challenges the place where they were in (ie, the wilderness), and the people in number (ie. 4000). Both writers of the account focus on these two issues, (Matthew adds in his account the words of the disciples "so great a multitude". The place as completely unfit for the challenge, and so is this world, and the multitude so great in number, yet the Saviour came to save the lost of this world, an even greater number.

2. The seeking of a sign by the religious leaders causes the Saviour much distress so as to warn the disciples of the leaven of the Pharisees. Bread is again the focus of the event, Mark stating the lack of bread, having only one loaf in the ship, whereas they had with them the 'Bread of Life'. The rebuke of the Saviour to their lack of understanding was that they might see the truth concerning the doctrine of the Pharisees and the Sadducees.

3. The event of the healing of the blind man is appropriate here since it concerned the necessity of understanding the words of the Saviour eg. 'be opened' in regard to the doctrine of the Pharisees and the Sadducees. This was tested by the challenge of the Lord as to His person, Peter being forthright in his confession 'Thou art the Christ' yet being faltering in his concept of the Saviour's purpose in coming into the world.

4. The final challenge to the people and the disciples is one that has far wider implications for the whole world.

'What will it profit a man if he gains the whole world and loses his own soul'. This is still applicable today and challenges the whole of mankind as to the keeping of their lives for themselves and not being willing to give their life to the God of Heaven to secure their eternal destiny.

MARK – CHAPTER 9

This chapter begins with the transfiguration of Jesus and ends with entry into the kingdom of God rather than being cast into hell. The teaching regarding the coming of Elijah, the healing of the man with the dumb spirit, status in the kingdom of God and lessons regarding childlike faith, all combine to give instruction as to the requirements for entry into the kingdom.

Divisions of the chapter:

V's 1– 8 – The transfiguration of Jesus
V's 9 – 13 – The teaching regarding Elijah
V's 14 – 29 – Trust and belief
V's 30 – 37 – True ambition

V's 1 – 8 Transfiguration of Jesus

   (i)   The favoured ones – Peter, James and John – Joined together – v2

   (ii)   The failure to perceive – Peter – Judging wrongly – v5

   (iii) The Father from heaven – Jehovah's voice – v 7

   (iv) The First and the Last – Jesus only – v 8

V's 9 – 13 Teaching regarding Elijah

   (i)   Why say the scribes? – False deduction – v 11

   (ii)   Elias has already come – Fulfilment arrived – v 13

V's 14 – 29 Trust and belief

- (i) The question posed – The challenge given – v 16
- (ii) The father's complaint – The complete failure – v 18
- (iii) The Lord reply – The condemnation – v 19
- (iv) The son brought – The command obeyed v 19
- (v) The plea put to the Lord – The compassion requested v 22
- (vi) The exercise of Faith – The culmination reached – v 27

V's 30 – 39 True ambition

- (i) A dispute arises – Seeking status – v's 33 /34
- (ii) A directive given – Simple lesson – v's 36/37
- (iii) A declaration issued – Submit humbly – v 37

V's 39 – 50 Transition to the Kingdom

- (i) An act forbidden – work in the Name – verse 39
  – An act favoured cleansing effect – welfare in the name – verse 41
- (ii) An act figurative – warning in the name – verses 42 – 50

CHAPTER 9 –

POINTS TO NOTE

1. The transfiguration was a unique experience for Peter, James and John and it is interesting to note the emphasis placed by each gospel writer. Mark says less about the change in Person of the Lord, but more about the change in raiment 9 Chapter 9 v 3. Luke says 'His raiment was white. (glistening) Matthew says 'His raiment became white as light'.

2. The timing of the transfiguration was registered by Mark as 'after six days' which seems to conflict with Luke's record, but it is not so. The significance of the 'six days' is intended to convey the time of creation and what is to follow ie. the fall of man, his redemption, and ultimate translation to glory.

3. The appearance of Moses and Elijah is mentioned by all the gospel writers but Mark places Elijah first and Moses second in contrast to Matthew and Luke. It would seem appropriate that such is the case because Elijah went from this world in a blaze of glory whilst Moses left with God alone to witness his exodus.

4. The healing of the child who was demon possessed required two things; 'Belief' on the part of the father of the child, and also 'belief' on the part of the disciples. Mark does not mention this in regard to the disciples but simply refers to the words of the Lord concerning 'Prayer and Fasting' Matthew, in his account states 'it was due to the unbelief of the disciples' that they experienced failure to heal the child, whilst the Father of the child confessed 'Lord I believe'.

5. A salutary lesson is given in the closing verses of this chapter. Whilst the disciples debated as to who was the greatest, the Lord took a child to give an example of simple trust. The desire for greatness rests in the willingness to remove that which offends, hence the need for 'Salt' to have that

MARK – CHAPTER 10

This chapter deals with those everyday concerns that befall human experience eg. Divorce, Childlike faith, everlasting life, fickleness, suffering, status, sacrifice and healing.

Main divisions of the chapter:

V's 1 – 12 – Divorce and disbelief
V's 13 – 16 – Displeasure and destiny
v's 17 – 27 – Desire and decision
V's 28 – 31 – Diplomacy and dedication
V's 32 – 45 – Death and displeasure
V's 46 – 52 – Desperation and delight

V's 1 – 12 Divorce and disbelief

    (i)   Tempting the Saviour – Misusing the Word – v 2

    (ii)   Telling the Truth – Making disobedience acceptable – v 5

    (iii) Two made one – Made to order – v 8

    (iv) Ties broken due to sin – Matters of human requirements v 11/12

V's 13 – 16 – Displeasure and destiny

    (i)   The disciples rebuked – Suffer the children – v 14

    (ii)   The Divine response – Such is of the kingdom – v 14

    (iii) The directive registered – Simple faith – v 16

V's 17 – 27 – An urgent matter – Eternal life – its obtaining

    (i)   An utterance contested – Extrication – all observed

(ii)   An unsettling challenge – Exemplification – Sell all – give

(iii) An unwilling spirit – Execution – he had great possessions

(iv)   An unthinkable outcome – Extraordinary – disciples astonished

(v)   An unlimited truth – Exposition – With God ALL

V's 28 – 31 Diplomacy and dedication.

(i)   A reminder given – Sacrifice

(ii)   A reward promised – Suerty

(iii) A record judged – Summing up

V's 32 – 45 Death and displeasure –

(i)   The path to be trod – Revelation

(ii)   The position to be desired – Recognition

(iii) The purpose to be fulfilled – Resolution

V's 46 –52 Desperation and delight

(i)   The person – The beggar – v 46

(ii)   The plight – The blindness – v's 47/48

(iii) The power – The beneficence – v 52

(iv)   The pursuit – The beginner – v 52

CHAPTER 10 –
POINTS TO NOTE

1. Mark reveals for us the direct challenge of the Pharisees regarding 'divorce', as does Matthew, but Luke confines this to one verse (see Luke chapter 16 verse 18). Mark makes no exemption for the action of divorce whilst Matthew gives only one exemption ie. 'fornication', which in the old testament is linked with 'idolatry'.

2. The episode of the rich young ruler is registered by all three gospel writers. Mark focusses on the fact that the young man has a great love for his riches. Jesus says "How hardly shall they that have riches enter into the kingdom of God" (repeated in Luke chapter 18).

3. Sacrifice and its reward is the concern of Peter, as Mark records, whilst 'position in the kingdom' was the concern of John and James, but what weighed heavy in the heart of the Lord was His impending death. It seems the disciples were more concerned with their rewards for the sacrifice they had made in following Christ, than for the great sacrifice of the Saviour, in obeying the FATHER'S WILL, by His death upon the cross, to redeem mankind from eternal damnation.

MARK – CHAPTER 11

The chapter brings before us various events occurring as the Lord and the disciples make their way to Jerusalem. There is the intercourse between the Lord and the chief priests, scribes and elders which closes the chapter, but in between are the riding into the city, the cleansing of the temple and the Exhortation of the Lord to His own concerning faith and prayer.

Division of the chapter:

V's 1 – 7 The procuring of the colt/ass
V's 8 – 10 The praise of the people
V's 11 – 14 The promise without the produce
V's 15 – 21 The profit in place of prayer
V's 22 – 26 The prayer of faith and its product
V's 27 – 33 The prejudice and perception

V's 1 – 7 The procuring of the colt/ass

    (i)   Go into the village – A directive v 2

    (ii)   Give an answer – A declaration v 3

    (iii)   Garments cast – A dedication v 7

V's 8 – 10 The praise of the people

    (i)   The recognition – Homage given v 8

    (ii)   The raised voices – Hallelujahs raised v 9

    (iii)   The rejoicing – Hope embraced v 10

V's 11 – 14 Promise without produce

    (i)   The fig tree – Seeing a fig tree v 13

    (ii) The fig leaves – Showing fruitfulness v 13

    (iii) The fruitlessness – Superficial display v 13

    (iv) The final word – Sad condition (generation) v 14

V's 15 – 21 Profit in place of prayer

    (i)   A conscious act – Exploitation judged v 15

    (ii) A cleansing act – Expellable action v 15

    (iii) A condemnatory word – Expressed wrath v 17

    (iv) A clear purpose – Ensure use v 18

V's 22 – 26 Prayer and its product

    (i)   Exhortation to Faith – Genuine guidance v 22

    (ii) Example of True prayer – Great things

    (iii) Effect of forgiveness – Graciousness

V's 27 – 33 Prejudice and perception

    (i)   A question contrived – Trickery

    (ii) A question controlled – Truth

    (iii) A quiet reasoning – Testing

    (iv) A qualified answer – Tactics

V 26

The beginning of this chapter deals with the parable of the vineyard and is followed by the question of tribute to Caesar and the problem of remarriage in eternity/kingdom. Then comes one scribe with the question relating to the greatest commandment. The chapter closes with doctrine in relation to David and the son of David and the widow's mite.

CHAPTER 11 –
POINTS TO NOTE

1. The procuring of the colt, as recorded by Mark, desinates the entry into Jerusalem for the second time, referred to as the 'triumphal entry', whereas the pervious entry upon an ass was unheralded. (see E. W. Bullinger – The two entries). Other commentators differ from this seeing only one entry. One thing is certain and that is that the Lord would have fulfilled, in detail, the prophecy of Zechariah chapter 9 verse 9 and used the two animals, the ass and the colt.

2. The cleansing of the temple is more detailed in Matthew and Mark than in Luke. Luke is very brief containing only the quote of the Lord concerning the 'house' Whereas Matthew and Mark focus on the profanity of the religious leaders in their actions and the emptiness of their 'so called' worship. This was akin to the fig tree with leaves, an outward show, but no real 'fruit'. Promise without Produce and Profit in place of Prayer'.

3. The challenge to the religious leaders in answer to their challenge about 'authority' is revealing, insomuch as their opinion relating to the 'Baptist's' testimony was put the test and they had no answer.' The Saviour thus put to silence their 'so called' accusation as to His authority and teachings.

MARK – CHAPTER 12

Divisions of the chapter:

V's 1 – 12 The wicked husbandmen
V's 13 – 17 The wanton hypocrisy
V's 18 – 34 The wilful neglect
V's 35 – 40 The wise challenge
V's 41 – 44 The widows mite

V's 1 –12 The wicked husbandmen

    (i)   The vineyard prepared – Privilege – v 1

    (ii)   The visits of the servants – Protocol – v 2

    (iii) The visitation of the Son – Principle – v 6

    (iv) The vile act – Profanity – v 8

    (v)   The violent end – Punishment v 9

V's 13 – 17 The wanton hypocrisy

    (i)   The plan to catch – Subtlety – v 13

    (ii)   The political challenge – Subterfuge – v 14

    (iii) The perception of the Lord – Sensitivity – v 15

    (iv) The penny brought – Symbolism – v 16

V's 18 – 34 The wilful neglect

    (i)   Earthly ties and the resurrection – Misunderstanding – v 24

(ii)   Error and ignorance – Misinterpretation – v 25

(iii) Eternal states – Miscalculation – v 25

(iv)   Error in magnitude – Misguided – v 26

V's 35 – 40 The wise challenge

(i)   Mystery relating to David – Truth declared – v 35

(ii)   Materialism of all the leaders – Timely wisdom – v 38

V's 41 – 44 The widow's mite

(i)   The casting in of money – Limited giving

(ii)   The call to the disciples – Lesson given

(iii) The commendation – Little but all

CHAPTER 12 –
POINTS TO NOTE

1. The parable of the wicked husbandmen is one that the enemies of the Lord were quick to interpret as being of them and their rejection of God's purposes in Christ. Mark gives us greater detail than Matthew or Luke, concerning the servants sent and the treatment they received. The sending of the Son is recorded by all the gospel writers but it is Mark and Luke who record 'my beloved Son' emphasising the desire of the owner of the vineyard to receive 'the fruit' from the husbandmen, to whom He gave the vineyard, but received nothing but hatred, rebellion, greed and self gain.

2. The lesson of the rejection of the 'stone' ie. 'the beloved Son' was to be judged in the most decisive way ie. 'miserable destruction', which followed, in the nation being scattered, for some 2000 years, without country, religious centre, or recognition as a nation, this being stated as 'the Lord's doing'. The 'kingdom' says Matthew, will be taken from them and given to another.

3. The incident relating to the tribute, combined with the events that followed, sought to 'catch the Saviour in his words' ie. the resurrection and the commandments. All these were answered in the light of what scripture stated and the result was 'no man asked any question of Him after this'.

4. The widow's mite was to teach the lesson of 'sacrificial giving', and is apt at this point, since the disciples were to learn the lesson that it was not the amount given that was important, but what the giver had left, so that the reasons and efforts of men fall short in their attempts to serve God from their own reasoning and success but simply the action of self denial was registered by God.

MARK – CHAPTER 13

This chapter is unique in content within the gospel, since it deals with future events and gives warning of those things that will occur at the end of days as determined by the statement in verse 10 of the chapter and its accomplishment.

Divisions of the chapter:

V's1 – 6 – The Enquiry
V's 7 – 8 – The End
V's 9 20 – The Elect
V's 21 – 27 – The Events
V's 28 –32 – The Exhortation

V's 1– 6 – The Enquiry – Curiosity

    (i)   When? – Time

    (ii)   What? – Testament

    (iii)   Watch! – Trouble

V's 7 – 8 – The End Not yet – Culmination

    (i)   Rumours – Warning

    (ii)   Rioting – Wantoness

    (iii)   Ruin – Wreckage

V's 9 – 20 – The Elect – Chosen

    (i)   For My Sake – Testimony

    (ii)   For My Name's sake Title

    (iii)   For the Elects sake Trouble

V's 21 –27 The Events – Collection
- (i) False claims – Deceit
- (ii) Further revelation – Declaration
- (iii) Future glory – Delight

V's 28 – 38 The Exhortation Command
- (i) Learn the Parable – Fig tree v 28
- (ii) Lasting words – Fulfilment v 30
- (iii) Look intently – Fasten

CHAPTER 13 –
POINTS TO NOTE

1. It is interesting that Mark singles out the four apostles who ask these questions relating to future events, since the same four apostles are mentioned at the beinning of Mark, s gospel when they were first called by the Lord. Mark here is careful in detail, as he is elsewhere in his writings.

2. The focus of the conversation is 'when shall these things be'?, and what shall be the 'sign' preceding these things? Matthew adds the words 'and the end of the world'.

3. The detail that the Lord gives seems to be more general rather than specific as to time, which indicates that, in light of what He declares concering the stones of the temple and destruction coming on Jerusalem the revelations are imminent but also can be referred to future days.

4. The declaration concerning the tribulation, not only a time of trouble for Jerusalem and the Jewish people, which was imminent, but a future tribulation such has not been seen since the beginning of creation, with devastating effects, that are global and in the heavens.

5. God will shorten these days, as is recorded by Matthew and Mark, but not Luke, the reason being that the devestation and desrtuction involved, is of such magnitude that no flesh shall be saved, but for the 'elects sake' the days will be shortened.

MARK – CHAPTER 14

This chapter covers a wide variety of actions by individuals and groups, from the anointing, to the Passover, to the betrayal and eventually to the denial and condemnation.

Divisions of the chapter:

V's 1 – 11 The anointing – A good work
V's 12 – 21 The assembling – A grave declaration
V's 22 – 31 The act – A gracious revelation
V's 32 – 41 The agony – A grievous load
V's 42 – 52 The abandonment – A growing fear
V's 53 – 65 The acquiescence – A gentle spirit
V's 66 – 72 The accusation – A genuine recognition

V's 1 – 11 The anointing – A good work

    (i)   There came a woman – Adoration v 3

    (ii)   There was indignation – Accusation v 4

    (iii)   There was commendation – Approval v 6

V's 12 – 21 The assembling – A grave declaration

    (i)   The Passover – Deliverance v 16

    (ii)   The problem – Deceit v 18

    (iii)   The person – Denunciation

V's 22 – 31 The Act – A gracious revelation

    (i)   My body given – The cross v 22

(ii)   My blood shed – The covenant v 24

(iii) My future hope – The coming v 25

V's 32 – 41 The Agony – A grievous load

(i)   Weighed down – The sin of the world v 33

(ii)   Will of the Father – The soul's obedience v 36

(iii) Wilful betrayal – The sinister plot v 41

V's 42 – 52 The abandonment – A growing fear

(i)   The token given – Fateful v 44

(ii)   The traitors kiss – False v 45

(iii) The traumatic effect – Fear

V's 53 – 65 The acquiescence – A gentle spirit

(i)   Fabricated witness – Conspiracy v 55

(ii)   Found peaceful – Control v 61

(iii) Flagrant condemnation – Consensus v 72

V's 66 – 72 The accusation A genuine recognition

(i)   One of them – Recognition v's 69/70

(ii)   Outright denial – Rebuff v's 69/70/71

(iii) Open weeping – Reflection v 72

CHAPTER 14 –
POINTS TO NOTE

1. The anointing of the Lord by the unnamed woman, as recorded by Mark, caused consternation among those who witnessed this act, His disciples, Judas, and others. Mark records the reaction by declaring 'there were some' that had indignation. Matthew declares pointedly that the disciples had indignation. Judas is to the forefront in this.

2. The act of betrayal was in the mind of Judas as they assembled for the feast of Passover. The Lord makes known what was to take place in accordance with the scripture record (see Psalm 41 verse 9); Judas was privileged to partake of the meal as Mark records (see verses 18 & 20) but was soon to leave and scripture records that 'he went out' and it was night (see John ch. 13 verse 26 – 30).

3. There follows the act of the 'last supper' and Jesus takes the bread and the wine to reveal to His own His impending death. Both Matthew and Mark make reference to the 'smiting of the shepherd' but not so Luke (see Zechariah ch. 13 verse 7)

4. Gethsemane was the place where the anticipation of the cross and 'the bearing of the sin of the whose world' engulfed the Saviour's person, that His sweat became as it were 'drops of blood falling to the ground', being in an 'agony of soul' in such an hour the disciple slept and Matthew and Mark stress that 'three times' the Lord found it to be the case hence the rebuke "What could you not watch with me one hour"?

5. Both Matthew and Mark record the 'forsaking' of the disciples leaving then Lord alone, Luke does not record this, but Mark, significantly, records that, 'a certain young man followed'. Conjecture as to who this was has been made by many, among whom there are those who say it was Mark. It is only here we have reference to this occurrence.

6. Matthew and Luke record the fact that they 'led Jesus away' whilst Mark says 'they took Him' and led Him. The disciples wanted to retaliate with the sword but Jesus acted with controlled spirit knowing that the scripture as being fulfilled, 'thus it is written' (see ch. 14 verse 49). The collaboration of the false witnesses is recorded by Matthew and Mark but Jesus 'held His peace', knowing gain that the scripture was being fulfilled.

Peter, though following after the multitude, was challenged on three occasions and denied the Lord each time fulfilling the prediction of the Lord.

The chapter begins with worship and ends with weeping, such is the case in humankind where those who believe worship and those who do not believe ultimately weep.

MARK – CHAPTER 15

This chapter details the arrest, trial and crucifixion of the Saviour, closing with the courage of Joseph of Arithamea begging the body of Jesus, and the Mary's looking on as He was laid in the tomb.

Divisions of the chapter:

V's 1 – 15 Before Pilate
V's 16 – 21 Bitter hatred
V's 22 – 39 Blatant mocking
V's 40 – 47 Bold action

V's 1 – 15 Before Pilate – Vacillation – Quote: He was manifestly superior, morally, to His judge. – W Kelly

   (i)   What will you have me do? – Concession v 12

   (ii)   Willing to content the people – Compliance v 15

   (iii) Whipping (scourging) Jesus – Convenience v 15

V's 16 – 21 Bitter hatred – Vileness – Quote: The action of the Jews had been venomous hatred. – W. Barclay

   (i)   Malice – Spitting v 19

   (ii)   Mugging – Shame v 18

   (iii) Mocking – Scorn v 20

V's 22 – 39 Blatant mocking – Vice – Quote: All of the soldiers wanted to enjoy the mocking of the Lord being King. – J. Heading

   (i)   Golgotha – The place v 22

(ii)   Garments – The possessions v 24

(iii) Great darkness – The Power v 33

(iv)   Gentile testimony – The perception

V's 40 – 47 Bold action – Valour – Quote: The special divine interposition with respect to our Lord's burial must not be overlooked. – J. A. Alexander

(i)   Craved the body – Concern v 43

(ii)   Clothed the body – Compassion v 46

(iii) Committed the body – Carefulness v 46

CHAPTER 15 –
POINTS TO NOTE

1. Mark's account of the Lord before Pilate is brief and to the point. He does not include the incidental occurrences such as Pilate's wife's intrusion, or the sending to Herod, or Judas's departure, as does the other gospel writers.
2. Matthew and Mark record the words of Pilate "Why what evil has He done"?, whilst Luke records "I find no fault in Him" but the people cried out the more "Crucify Him", moved with bitter hatred by the religious leaders.
3. The cry of the people concerning the Lord's execution is recorded only by Matthew "His blood be on us and on or children."

MARK – CHAPTER 16

This chapter b rings to an end Mark's record with the visit of the women to the tomb, the appearing to Mary Magdalene, and then to the two on the road to Emmaus, and lastly to the disciples before His ascension to heaven.

Divisions of the chapter:

V's 1– 8 Anticipation
V's 9 – 18 Appearances
V's 19 – 20 Ascension

V's 1 – 8 Anticipation – Anointing – Quote: They knew they did not have the strength to roll the stone – J. Heading

   (i)   The stone rolled away – The barrier removed v 4

   (ii)   The sign that He is risen – The bizarre announcement v 6

   (iii)   The shock of the revelation – The bewilderment v 8

V's 9 – 18 Appearances – Assurance – Quote He reproached them for their unbelief and hardness of heart, because they had not believed those who had seen Him risen. W. Kelly. –

   (i)   To the demon possessed – The first day v 9

   (ii)   To the two disciples – The form changed v 12

   (iii)   To the eleven – The failure to believe v 14

V's 19 – 20 Ascension Awaiting _ Quote: The right hand here denotes the place of Honour and delegated power. – J. A. Alexander

   (i)   His position – At the right hand v 19

   (ii) Their preaching – To reach out v's 15/20

CHAPTER 16 –
POINTS TO NOTE

1. Mark is careful to record the names of those women going to the sepulchre, but Luke tells us of others that accompanied them. The purpose was to anoint the body with spices.

2. One problem that confronted them was the 'rolling away of the stone', for Mark tells us it was 'very great'. Matthew gives us the answer to this, declaring that an angel of the Lord descended and 'rolled b ack the stone' (see Matthew ch. 25 verse 2).

3. Mark repeats the details of the reaction of the women declaring 'they were afraid' (verse 4 & 8) and they went out quicky and fled from the sepulchre.

4. Mark tells us of the encounter with Mary Magdalene, but only briefly, for a more detailed account see John chapter 20 verses 11 – 17.

5. On her return to the disciples to reveal that she had 'seen the Lord', she was not believed, the disciples saying it was 'idle tales' (see Luke chapter 24 v

6. The Lord appears to the eleven, after the encounter with the two on their way to Emmaus, to whom He revealed himself, and upbraids the disciples for their 'unbelief'. Mark tells us tells us of the 'great commission' recording the words of the Saviour "Go ye into all the world and preach the gospel to every creature" And they went forth and preached everywhere.

OUTLINES IN THE GOSPEL OF LUKE

[1]The gospel of Luke – presentation of Christ as God's perfect man

The account given by Luke, the physician, looks at the life, ministry death and resurrection of the Son on Man. but no less than the Son of God, and His ministry as such which contained so many features that relate to human situations, depicting human reactions, often including human responses, and creating human opinions and divisions. Luke is careful to note these and record them as a physician would be trained to do.

LUKE – CHAPTER 1

HUMANITY GETS CONFIRMATION

1. Introduction – certainty of things taught – verses 1 – 4
2. Birth of John the Baptist – You will have a son – verses 5 – 17
3. Jesus's birth foretold – The holy Spirit shall come – verses 18 – 36
4. Mary visits Elizabeth – Blessed are you – verses 37 – 45
5. Mary's song – The mighty one has done great things – verses 46 – 56
6. Birth of John the Baptist – His name is John – verses 57 – 66
7. Zechariah's song – Prophet of the most high – verses 67 – 80

(a)   Luke writes to confirm the things taught

(i) Those who were eyewitnesses of those things.

(ii) I too, so that you may know the certainty of the things you have been taught.

(b) Birth of John the Baptist

  (i) Gabriel sent to confirm the birth of John.

  (ii) Do not be afraid your prayer has been heard.

  (iii) Your wife Elizabeth will bear a son.

  (iv) He will be called John.

  (v) He will be filled with the Holy Spirit.

  (vi) He will go before the Lord in the spirit of Elijah.

  (vii) To make ready a people prepared for the Lord.

LUKE – CHAPTER 2

LUKE CHAPTER 2 BIRTH OF JESUS – DETAILS – HUMAN ACTIVITIES OF EVERYDAY LIFE – V'S1–21

(1) Jesus as a boy in the Temple – The Father's business – verses 40 – 51

(1) Birth of Baby son –. ——— FACT

　(i)　Now Joseph went up to Bethlehem with Mary his wife and she gave birth to her firstborn and call his name Jesus

　(ii)　There were Shepherds in the fields – angels appeared to them

　(iii)　Told them a Saviour had been born – Jesus – the Christ.

　(iv)　They made their way to the manger – found the child – worshipped Him

　(v)　They went into the city to tell what they had seen and heard – The good news has started to be made known through men of basic occupation.

(2) The next reference we have is the taking of the child to the temple to be presented to then Lord according to the Law. —— FULFILLMENT

    (i) Having entered the temple there was a man waiting, named Simeon, waiting for the consolation of Israel, who seeing the child, took him in his arms and Expressed his delight in a prayer to God declaring "Mine eyes have seen YOUR SALVATION".

    (ii) Simeon was an expectant believer of the promise that God would send a 'deliverer', to be known as Messiah.

    (iii) Also present was Anna, a prophetess, and a widow of many years, went and spoke to all in Jerusalem who looked for REDEMPTION in ISRAEL.

    (iv) Luke thus tells us of the spreading of the good news, starting in Jerusalem, and subsequently throughout the whole world.

(3) Jesus as a boy in the temple. —— FIDELITY

    (i) The boy Jesus decided to stay behind in the temple.

    (ii) His parents thought He was in the company.

    (iii) After three days of searching they found Him in the temple.

    (iv) He was debating with the teachers of the Law.

    (v) Everyone was amazed at His understanding.

    (vi) After his parents told Him of the search they had undertaken – he replied – "Dont you know I must be about MY FATHER'S BUSINESS".

Mary treasured all these things in her heart.
Jesus presented in the temple.

    (i) The law kept – every male firstborn – presented

(ii)   Simeon was an expectant believer of the Promise

(iii)   Mine eyes have seen your Salvation

(iv)   Anna spoke to all in Jerusalem who Looked for REDEMPTION.

LUKE – CHAPTER 3

1. John the Baptist – Prepare the Way – The voice – verses 1 – 20
2. The baptism of Jesus
3. The genealogy of Jesus

(1) John the Baptist – The voice in the wilderness —— REPENTANCE

   (i)   John came preaching the baptism of repentance.

   (ii)   Every tree not bearing fruit – cut down – thrown into fire.

   (iii)   People ask "What should they do"?

   (iv)   John declared the good news to them.

   (v)   Herod imprisons John.

(2) The baptism of Jesus and His genealogy – RIGHTEOUSNESS ——

   (i)   Lukes's account of the Baptism the briefest.

   (ii)   Jesus was baptised to fulfil righteousness.

   (iii)   Whilst praying the voice came from Heaven.

   (iv)   The genealogy of Jesus – the son of David, Abraham, Adam, God.

(3) The genealogy of Jesus —— ROOTS

   (i)   the son of Joseph —— so thought

   (ii)   the son of David, the son of Abraham

   (iii)   the Son of God

LUKE – CHAPTER 3

1. John the Baptist – Prepares the Way – verses 1 – 20
2. The baptism of Jesus – The Son of God – verses 21 – 37

(1) John was predicted to be the voice in the 'wilderness' preparing the way of the Lord (see Isaiah ch. 40 verses 3 – 11) ⸺ REPENTANCE

   (i) John was looking for the fruit of 'repentance' from Kings, rulers and the common people.

  (ii) Thus he was preaching the 'baptism of repentance'

 (iii) Every tree not bearing fruit would be cut down and thrown in the fire.

(2) The baptism of Jesus – The Son of God. ⸺ RIGHTEOUSNESS

   (i) Jesus comes to John to be baptized

  (ii) John declares "I have need to be baptized of you"

 (iii) Whilst praying 'the dove descends and the voice is heard

 (iv) An even greater voice than that of John – A voice from heaven

  (v) The ultimate authority – God Himself – 'This is my BELOVED SON' – Man is still looking for the ultimate 'Authority' to rule in the affairs of the world

 (vi) He 'the Lamb, the King, the Messiah, must, as John declares, INCREASE and I must decrease

(vii) Triune witness – Father, Son and Holy Ghost

LUKE – CHAPTER 4

1. The testing of Jesus – Temptation – verses 1 – 13
2. Jesus rejected at Nazareth – His own city – verses 14 – 37
3. Jesus heals many – Simon's mother in law – verses 38 – 44

(1) The testing of Jesus – Temptation —— RECOMMENDATION

  (i) On three fronts – Bodily needs – Spiritual worship – Devotion to God

  (ii) Temptation – 40 days – victory gained through the 'written word' (see verse 5)

  (iii) It was Satan's voice that suggested the 'Temptation' – Command that these stones

  (iv) It did not come from inward desire within the Lord.

  (v) It did not yield the result that Satan desired

(2) Jesus rejected at Nazareth – His own city —— REJECTION

  (i) The Lord comes to Nazareth where He Had been brought up

  (ii) The Lord sought to teach in their synagogues – two examples – Naaman – Widow

  (iii) They were offended and sought to lay hands on Him

(3) Jesus heals many – Despite rejection –––– REPUTATION

   (i)   The people of His own city REJECT Him

   (ii) They said "What have we to do with you"

   (iii) Verse 41 – The very devils ACKNOWLEDGE HIM

   (iv) The fame of the Lord spread quickly

   (v)   The Lord left the synagogue – entered the house of Peter's mother in law. – He heals her and she ministers to them

The examples demonstrate the contrast of belief as against BLATENT UNBELIEF – they drove Him out and took Him to the top of the hill.

Familiarity coloured their thinking – pride dominated their actions.

LUKE – CHAPTER 5

1. Jesus calls His first disciples – Simon Peter etc. – verses 1 – 12
2. Jesus heals the paralysed man – verses 13 – 16
3. Jesus forgives and heals the paralysed man – verse 17 –26
4. Jesus calls Levi. – verses 27 – 31
5. Jesus questioned about fasting – verses 32 – 39

(1) Jesus calls His first disciples. ——— a call to FOLLOW

    (i) When Jesus was standing by the lake of Gennesaret He saw two boats.

    (ii) He got into one boat, which was Simon's, and asked him to pull a little from the shore

    (iii) Jesus then taught the people.

    (iv) When He had finished speaking, He said to Peter "Pull out to deep water and let down the nets"

    (v) When they obeyed they caught such a large number that their boats began to sink.

    (vi) Peter was overcome and cried out "Depart from me for I am a sinful man"

    (vii) The Lord answered do not be afraid from now on you will fish for people

(2) Jesus heals the Leper' ——— a cleansing to be FELT The man came begging for the Lord to heal him but doubting His willingness to do so

   (i) The Lord answered his request immediately with His I will.

   (ii) The Saviour commanded him to tell no one.

   (iii) The man went and spread abroad what Jesus had done.

(3) Jesus calls Levi. ——— a call to be FREE

   (i) Jesus saw a tax collector – There is no selective choice here – God looks only at the heart.

   (ii) Jesus simply says "follow me"– those words triggered something in the heart of Levi.

   (iii) He immediately left all and obeyed.

   (iv) He then laid on a great banquet for the Lord – Who attended, despite the criticism of the Pharisees etc.

   (v) Levi or Matthew was later to be used by God for the writing of the gospel.

(4) Jesus called to account for His disciples activities. ——— a call to FELLOWSHIP

   (i) John's disciples, so too the Pharisees disciples, fast, but yours do not'

   (ii) Jesus answered "Can you make the friends of the bridegroom 'fast' when He is with them"?

   (iii) He then tells then, by parable, of a new era entering into Israel.

LUKE – CHAPTER 6

1. Jesus is Lord of the Sabbath – verses 1 – 12
2. The twelve apostles – named – verses 13 – 16
3. Blessings and Woes – verses 17 – 26
4. Love your enemies – verses 27 – 36
5. Judging others – verses 37 – 42 — Judge not
6. A tree and its fruits – verses 43 – 45 — Good & bad
7. Wise and foolish builders – verses 46 – 49 — Foundations

(1) Jesus is Lord of the Sabbath. ——— POSITION

   (i) This was the second sabbath referred to by Luke as one sabbath.

   (ii) There are several incidents recorded by Luke that took place on sabbath days.

   (iii) See Exodus chapter 12 verse 16 – re; the seventh day

   (iv) The Lord answers them quoting David, see 1 Samuel chapter 26.

   (v) The Son of Man is Lord of the Sabbath.

(2) The twelve apostles – named ——— PREROGATIVE

   (i) Simon first and Judas last, with reference to Judas as a traitor.

   (ii) He chose twelve whom He designated as 'Apostles'

   (iii) He spent the night before in prayer.

(3) The blessings and woes ——— PRONOUNCEMENTS

   (i) His presence encouraged a large crowd to gather, He healed many, many sought to touch Him.

Looking at His disciples
       He said "Blessed are you who are poor etc."
  (ii)   He then pronounced woes.
  (iii) 'Woes' on the rich and indulgent in this life.

(4) Love for your enemies. ——— PACIFY
    (i)   Love your enemies. Do good to those who hate you, bless those who curse you, pray for those who ill treat you etc.
   (ii)   Do to others as you would have them do to you.
  (iii) Be merciful as your Father is merciful.

(5) Judging others. ——— PROBITY
    (i)   Do not judge others and you will not be judged.
   (ii)   Can the blind lead the blind?
  (iii) The example given is the speck and beam – where the obvious is ignored.

(6) A tree and its fruits. ——— PRODUCE
    (i)   Each tree is recognised by its own fruit.
   (ii)   Good tree – good fruit/bad tree – bad fruit
  (iii) A goodman produces good things/a bad man evil things.

(7) Wise and foolish building. ——— PENETRATION
    (i)   The foundation is all important when building.
   (ii)   The wise build on a rock foundation/the foolish on an unsure foundation – like sand
  (iv) When building for God the foundation is already laid – ie. Christ

Great is your reward in heaven.

LUKE CHAPTER 7

1. The faith of the centurion. – verses 1 – 10
2. Jesus raises the widow woman's son – verses 11 – 18
3. Jesus and John the Baptist – verses 19 – 35
4. Jesus anointed by the sinful woman – verses 36 – 50

(1) The faith of the centurion. ――― SINCERITY

   (i) The centurion was a Roman officer over a garrison.

   (ii) The centurion was morally responsible – He loved his servant.

   (iii) The Jews said he was worthy.

   (iv) He loves our nation – has built us a synagogue.

   (v) The centurion did not consider himself worthy to approach the Lord.

   (vi) He said "speak the word only" – that is sufficient.

   (vii) The Lord replied "I have not found so great faith 'not in Israel"

(2) Jesus raises the widow woman's son. ――― SURPRISE

   (i) The Lord knew what He would do (see chapter 22 verse 60)

   (ii) The Lord was moved with compassion – evidence of His humanity

   (iii) Treatment of widows generally was lacking in compassion – (see Ezekiel ch. 22 v 27 & Malachi ch. 3 v 5)

(iv) The Saviour said "weep not" – H e shared her sorrow.

(v) "Young man I say to you arise" – words of authority

(vi) The people were all filled with awe.

(3) Jesus and John the Baptist. – John knew thar Jesus was —— SURETY

  (i) The Messiah – all flesh shall see the 'salvation of God' (Luke ch. 3 v 6)

 (ii) He who would baptise with the ' Holy Spirit ' (Luke ch. 3 v 16).

(iii) He was the 'Lamb of God' (John ch. 1 v 29)

(iv) He was the 'Son of God' (John ch. 1 v 34)

 (v) He that comes from above is 'above all' (John ch. 3 v 31)

(vi) That grace and truth came by 'Jesus Christ' (John ch. 1 v 17)

John wanted confirmation – The Lord told John's disciples "Go and tell John what you have seen and heard"

The Lord explains the ministry of John.

(4) Jesus anointed by a sinful woman. —— SAGASITY

  (i) Distinct from the anointing of Mary of Bethany.

 (ii) The woman is identified as a 'sinner' – unnamed.

(iii) The 'humility' of the woman described in verse 38.

(iv) Simeon thought the Lord did not know of the woman.

 (v) A lesson in forgiveness and love was to be learned by Simeon.

LUKE – CHAPTER 8

(1) The parable of the Sower, ——— SOWING

   (i)   A farmer went out to sow seed.

   (ii)   The seed fell on path – trampled underfoot – birds ate them.

   (iii) Seed fell on rocky ground – no depth – withered.

   (iv)   Seed fell among thorns – choked.

   (v)   Seed fell on good ground – produced fruit.

(2) A lamp on a stand ——— SHINING

   (i)   No one lights a lamp and hides it. – light is needed to illumine the individual who is in darkness.

   (ii)   The hidden things will be revealed – and those things concealed will be brought into the open.

   (iii) Therefore consider carefully how you listen – with open mind or closed mind.

(3) Jesus's mother and brothers —— STATE

   (i) Those who hear My word and practice it are My mother and brother.

   (ii) The Lord calls us 'brethren' (see Matthew ch. 28 v 10, John ch. 29 v 17, Hebrews ch. 2 v's 11 – 13.

(4) Jesus calms the storm. —— SOVREIGNITY

   (i) The Lord's power over disease, disasters, demons, death etc.

   (ii) The Lord initiates the journey

   (iii) The Lord engages in sleep

   (iv) The storm arises, natural phenomena, the adversary, God? – Psalm 147 v 18

   (v) He stilled the storm to a whisper – Psalm 107 v 29

(5) Jesus restores a demon possessed man. —— SANITY

   (i) The man wore no clothes – open and naked. – as was Adam

   (ii) The man abode in the tombs – no house – death

   (iii) The demons said "Jesus, the Son of God" – not Lord

   (iv) Most High – Millenial Title – The Supreme Authority

   (v) What is your name? – Legion – for we are many

   (vi) Swine – uncleanness – where the demons wanted to go

   (vii) The Lord sent the man home – to WITNESS

(6) Jesus heals a sick woman / raises a girl from the dead —— SALVATION

   (i) Woman with issue of blood touches His coat edge.

(ii) Lord asks "who touched Me" – Peter refers to the crowd.

(iii) Woman knew she could not be hidden – confesses – faith commended.

(iv) Don't bother the teacher anymore – daughter has died.

(v) Lord says to Jairus "do not be afraid" – "Just believe"

(vi) In the house the Lord says "She is just asleep" and they laughed at Him – knowing she was dead.

(vii) The Lord said "child get up" – her spirit returned – she rose up and ate.

(viii) The parents ordered not to tell anyone.

LUKE – CHAPTER 9

1. Jesus sends out then twelve – verses 1 – 9
2. Jesus feeds the 5000 – verses 10 – 17
3. Peter declares Jesus as the Messiah – verses 18 – 22
4. Jesus predicts His death. – verses 23 – 27
5. The transfiguration – verses 28 – 36
6. Jesus heals the demon possessed boy – verses 37 – 43
7. Jesus predicts His death (2nd time) – verses 44 – 50
8. Samaritan opposition – verses 51 – 56
9. The cost of following Jesus – verses 57 – 62

(1) Jesus sends out the twelve ——— COMMISSION

   (i)   The focus here is a commission to service.

   (ii)   Such a commission needed 'Power and authority'

   (iii)   The ministry involved 'Preaching and healing of the sick'.

   (iv)   So they went out proclaiming the good news and healing.

   (v)   Herod was perplexed – thinking John the Baptist was raised from the dead.

(2) Jesus feeds the 5000 ——— COMPASSION

   (i)   On return the disciples reported what they had done.

   (ii)   Jesus welcomed the crowd and healed those in need.

   (iii)   Jesus feeds the crowd.

   (iv)   All ate and were satisfied.

(3) Peter declares Jesus as the Messiah —— CONFESSION

    (i)   The disciples are challenged by the Lord.

    (ii)   Peter confesses Jeus as Messiah.

(4) Jesus predicts His death. —— COST

    (i)   Jesus tells His disciples all that was going to happen.

    (ii)   Jesus declares the cost of discipleship.

    (iii) Jesus refers to those there who would see the kingdom.

(5) The transfiguration —— CHANGE

    (i)   The place – the mountain top.

    (ii)   The persons – Moses and Elijah.

    (iii) The purpose – My beloved Son.

    (iv) The privilege – to get a glimpse of the 'kingdom'.

    (v)   The precaution – tell no one.

(6) The demon possessed boy. —— CONDEMNATION

    (i)   A man called out of the crowd.

    (ii)   The disciples failed to heal.

    (iii) The Saviour issues a condemnation.

    (iv) Then heals the boy.

(7) Jesus predicts His death – 2nd, Time —— CONFIRMATION

    (i)   Argument among the disciples – who is the greatest – a child.

    (ii)   One who is the least – is greatest.

(8) Samaritan opposition. —— CONTEST

   (i)   As the time approached for Him to be taken back to heaven.

   (ii)   Jesus set out for Jerusalem.

   (iii) Those sent went to a Samaritan village.

   (iv) The Samaritans rejected Jesus – because He was headed to Jerusalem.

   (v)   John and James wanted to call fire down from heaven.

(9) Cost of discipleship. —— COST

   (i)   The Son of Man has no place to lay His head.

   (ii)   He said to another 'follow Me' – he was concerned with other things.

   (iii) Another wanted to say 'goodbye' to his family.

   (iv) No one who puts his hand to the plough and looks back is fit for service in the 'kingdom of God'.

LUKE – CHAPTER 10

(1) Jesus sends out His disciples.
(2) The parable of the good Samaritan.
(3) The home at Bethany.

    (i) He sent them two by two – Fellowship – support – testimony. —— COMISSION

    (ii) 10 x 7 – 10 – in scripture – number of Responsibility – 7 – in scripture number of spiritual completion.

    (iii) He is Lord of the harvest – harvest is plentiful – workers are few.

    (iv) Do not take 'purse or bag' – find a worthy person.

    (v) Reception – Welcome/not welcome – Enter into fellowship/Shake the dust off your feet.

    (vi) Chorazin – Bethsaida – Capernaum – Woes pronounced.

    (vii) The seventy returned with joy.

    (viii) Praise to the Father for revelation.

    (ix) Blessed are the eyes that see what you see.

(4) The parable of the good Samaritan. ——— COMPASSION

    (i) An expert in the law challenged Jesus.

    (ii) Jesus replied – "What does the law say"?

    (iii) Love the Lord your God and your neighbour as yourself.

   (iv) The expert asked "Who is my neighbour"?

   (v) A man was travelling down from Jerusalem to Jericho.

  (vi) Priest passed, Levite passed and a Samaritan stopped.

 (vii) Which of these three were a neighbour to him?

(viii) The one who showed him mercy.

  (ix) Go and do 'likewise'.

(5) The home at Bethany. ———— CHOICE

   (i) The home of Martha, Mary and Lazarus.

  (ii) Martha opened her home to Jesus.

 (iii) Mary sat at the feet of Jesus.

 (iv) Martha complained – tell Mary to help me.

  (v) Mary has chosen what is better.
The secular is set against THE SPIRITUAL – the spiritual is always to be primary – Man shall not live by 'bread alone'.

LUKE – CHAPTER 11

1. Jesus's teaching on Prayer. – verses 1 – 13
2. Jesus and Beelzebul. – verses 14 – 28
3. The sign of Jonah. – verses 29 – 32
4. The lamp of the body – verses 33 – 54

(1) Jesus's teaching on Prayer. —— TEACHING

   (i)   The disciples ask the Lord – "Teach us to pray"

   (ii) The Lord's prayer – Person – purpose – provision – pardon – protection

   (iii) The importunity of a friend – continuous knocking.

   (iv) Men aught always to pray (continuity) – Ask, knock, seek – Faith – God first continually. –

(2) Jesus and Beelzebul. —— TESTING

   (i)   The mute spoke – people amazed – accusation – by Beelzebul the prince of demons.

   (ii) The elders accuse – some wanted a sign.

   (iii) If Satan is divided how can his house stand?

   (iv) The casting out of the demons – Beelzebul – impossible – must be of God.

(3) Sign of Jonah. —— TRUTH

   (i)   The Jews sought a sign greater than the miracles.

   (ii) A wicked generation seeks a sign.

   (iii) Religious experience, based on a sign, not reliable.

   (iv) No sign given – but the sign of the prophet Jonah.

(v) Three days/nights – Saviour's death and resurrection.

(vi) Repentance is what God is looking for.

(4) The parable of the Lampstand. ——— TRANPARENCY

   (i) Light not to be 'Hidden'

   (ii) Nothing is hidden that shall not be revealed.

   (iii) To him that has more will be given/to him who has not – taken away.

(5) Woes pronounced. ——— TROUBLE

   (i) Woe to you Pharisees – you neglect justice and the Love of God.

   (ii) You love the most important seats in the synagogue.

   (iii) You are like unmarked graves.

   (iv) Your ancestors killed the prophets.

   (v) You load people with burdens they cannot bear.

   (vi) You have taken away the key to knowledge.

LUKE – CHAPTER 12

A Summary

Warnings and Encouragements ———— CAUTION

Chapter 12 of the Gospel of Luke begins with Jesus addressing a large crowd, cautioning them against the hypocrisy of the Pharisees. He emphasizes the importance of living in the truth, for nothing concealed will remain hidden. Jesus encourages his followers to fear God, who has the power over life and death, rather than fearing human judgment.

The Parable of the Rich Fool ———— CALAMITY

Jesus tells the story of a rich man whose land produced an abundant harvest. The man decides to build larger barns to store his surplus grain and take life easy, but God calls him a fool, as his life is demanded that very night. This parable illustrates the futility of earthly wealth and the importance of being rich toward God.

Do Not Worry ——— CONFIDENCE

Jesus instructs his disciples not to worry about their lives, what they will eat, or their bodies, what they will wear. He points to the ravens and the lilies, explaining that God provides for them and will surely provide for his people. He urges them to seek God's kingdom, and their needs will be met.

Watchfulness ——————— CONDITION

Jesus teaches the importance of being watchful and ready for the coming of the Son of Man. He uses the analogy of servants waiting for their master to return from a wedding banquet, emphasizing the being watchful.

Jesus criticizes the crowd for their ability to interpret the weather but their failure to understand the present times. He calls them to recognize the urgency of his message and the importance of making peace with their adversaries before it is too late.

Parable of the Faithful and Wise Manager ——————— CONSIENTIOUS

Jesus continues with a parable about a manager put in charge of the master's servants. The faithful and wise manager will be rewarded for their diligence, while the one who abuses their power will face severe punishment. This underscores the responsibility and accountability of those in positions of leadership. Not Peace, but Division.

NO PEACE BUT DIVISION ——————— CLEAVAGE

Jesus acknowledges that his message will cause division, even among families. He speaks of the fire he has come to bring on earth and the baptism of suffering he must undergo. He warns that following him may lead to conflict and separation.

Luke chapter 12 is a chapter filled with teachings on the importance of sincerity, the futility of materialism, the necessity of trust in God, and the call to be vigilant and prepared. Jesus' words challenge his followers to live with an eternal perspective, prioritizing God's kingdom above all else.

LUKE – CHAPTER 13

(1) Repent or Perish. —— REPENTANCE

  (i)   Galileans whom executed – blood used in sacrifice.

  (ii) Or those who died when the Tower of Siloam fell.

  (iii) I tell you unless you repent – you likewise will perish.

  (iv) A man had a fig tree – no fruit after three years – cut it down.

  (v)   Let it alone for a year – if no fruit – then cut it down

(2) Jesus heals a cripple on a sabbath day. —— REBUKE

  (i)   On a sabbath day – in a synagogue.

  (ii) A crippled woman – 18 years – could not straighten.

  (iii) Jesus saw her – called her forward.

  (iv) Jesus told her "Woman you are free from your infirmity."

  (v)   Jesus put His hands on her – she was cured.

  (vi) Hypocrites – You release your donkeys – should not this woman be released.

  (vii) All His opponents – humiliated.

(3) Parable of mustard seed and yeast. —— RELATION

    (i)   Kingdom of God – Like a mustard a tree.

    (iii)   Birds perched in its branches.

    (iv)   Kingdom of God – like yeast.

    (v)   Woman mixed about 30 kg.

    (vi)   Worked all through the dough.

(4) The narrow door —— RIGHTEOUS

    (i)   Are only a few people going to be saved?

    (ii)   Many will try to enter and not be able.

    (iii)   Once the door is closed.

    (iv)   There will be the 'cry' "open to us" – the answer "comes" I don't know you 'Leave this place'.

    (v)   There will be weeping and wailing and gnashing of teeth.

(5) Jesus's sorrow for Jerusalem. —— RUEFUL

    (i)   Leave this place – Herod seeks to kill you.

    (ii)   Jesus replied – "I must press on"

    (iii)   No prophet can die outside of Jerusalem.

    (iv)   The sorrow expressed – ''O Jerusalem. O Jerusalem

    (v)   Your house is left unto you DESOLATE

    (vi)   Until the time come —— Blessed is He who comes

LUKE – CHAPTER 14

1. Jesus at a Pharisees house.
2. Parable of the great banquet.
3. Cost of being a disciple.

(1) Jesus at a Pharisees house. —— REALITY

    (i) Jesus in the Pharisees house – dining

    (ii) The Pharisee was a prominent man.

    (iii) In front of Jesus was a man abnormally swollen.

    (iv) Jesus asks those present "Is it lawful to heal on a sabbath day"?

    (v) They remained silent

    (vi) If a child or an ox fell into a well you would pull it out.

    (v) They had nothing to say.

    (vii) When invited to a feast take the lowest seat'

    (viii) When you give a banquet invite the poor, crippled, lame and blind.

(2) Parab le of the great banquet. —— REFUSAL

    (i) Blessed is the one who eats at the 'Kingdom of God'.

    (ii) Prepared banquet – those invited all made excuses.

    (iii) Servant returned and told the master.

    (iv) Master reacted "go into the streets and highways".

    (v) Bring in the poor, crippled, lame and blind.

    (vi) Not one of those invited will get a taste.

(3) The cost of being a 'disciple' —— RESEARCH

  (i) The priority is Christ first – mother, brother, even life.

 (ii) Whoever does not carry their cross cannot follow.

(iii) Such cannot be My disciple.

 (iv) Project – building a tower – unfinished. – plan the cost – check resources – avoid ridicule.

 (vi) Salt, if it loses its flavour (saltiness) no longer useful.

(vii) King going to war – establish strength of the enemy – check resources – send a delegation to negotiate terms etc.

     Are you prepared to give up everything to be 'My disciple'?

LUKE – CHAPTER 15

1. The parable of the Lost sheep – Verses 1 – 7
2. The parable of the lost coin – verss 8 – 10
3. The parable of the lost son – verses 11 – 32

(1) The parable of the lost sheep. —— SEEKING

  (i)   The Pharisees and teachers of the Law – muttered against Jesus.

  (ii) Jesus told them this parable.

  (iii) The importance of one lost sheep.

  (iv) The effort expended to find it.

  (v)   The joy & rejoicing when it is found.

  (vi) (Rejoicing over one sinner that repents.

(2) The parable of the lost coin. —— SEARCHING

  (i)   A woman has 10 silver coins.

  (ii) She loses one of the ten.

  (iii) She sweeps the house – searches carefully.

  (iv) Until she finds it.

  (v)   Rejoice with me for I have found it.

(3) Parable of the lost son. —— SANGUINE

  (i)   Two sons – the younger son "give me my share of the estate".

  (ii) Father divided the estate between the two.

(iii)	The younger son decided to set out for the far country.
(iv)	Squandered his wealth on wild living.
(v)	After he spent everything a famine arose.
(vi)	He began to be in need.
(vii)	Found work – sent to feed the pigs.
(viii)	Ended up eating the pigs food.
(ix)	Came to his senses – my father's servants are better off than *I am*
(x)	I will arise and go to my father.
(xi)	While afar off the father saw him.
(xii)	Ran – fell on his neck and kissed him.
(xiii)	The son confessed his wayward ways.
(xiv)	The father ordered "bring the best robe" —— etc.
(xv)	This my son was lost and is found, was dead and is alive.
(xvi)	Elder son heard the rejoicing and was angry.
(xvii)	Complained to the father.
(xviii)	Son you are everything – all I have is yours
(xix)	We had to celebrate – your brother was lost/found, dead/alive.

LUKE – CHAPTER 16

1. The shrewd manager – verses 1 – 15
2. Additional teaching – verses 16 – 18
3. The rich man and Lazarus – verses 19 – 31

(1) The shrewd manager. ——— DISCERNMENT

   (i)   The shrewd steward realised his shortcomings.

   (ii)   He tried to repair the situation.

   (iii) By reaching out to his master's debtors.

   (iv) The reducing of the debts gain favour.

   (v)   The debts would be taken on by the shrewd steward.

   (vi) The worldly man is wiser than the believer.

   (vi) Using even scripture to advantage. The law and the prophets.

(2) Additional teaching. ——— DIRECTION

   (i)   The law and the prophets served their purpose.

   (ii)   The preaching of the kingdom of God replaced this.

   (iii) The misuse of this preaching by 'everyone forcing'.

   (iv) Divorce is set forth as an example.

   (iv) Heaven & earth will pass away before the law is abolished even though grace prevails.

(3) The rich man and Lazarus. —— DIVISION

   (i) There was a rich man – living a rich man's life.

  (ii) There was a beggar at his gate – covered in sores longing to eat.

 (iii) The beggar died ad went to Sheol (Paradise).

 (iv) The rich man died and went to Hades.

  (v) In Hades – the rich man could see Lazarus.

 (vi) Plead for Abraham to send Lazarus – drop of water.

(vii) Great gulf fixed – none can cross over.

(viii) I have five brothers – Send to them.

 (ix) They have Moses and the Prophets.

  (x) If they do not believe them neither will they believe though one rise from the dead.

Opportunities passed by will in a coming day condemn. Such the rich man had every day, he wanted to act on behalf o family but they had the same 'opportunity' as the rich man.

LUKE – CHAPTER 17

1. Sin – faith – duty.
2. Jesus heals ten men of Leprosy.
3. The coming kingdom of God.

(1) Sin – faith – duty. —— RESPONSIBILITY

   (i)   Do not cause stumbling – these little ones. – So watch yourselves.

  (ii) Sin against you – 7 times – Forgiveness. – On repentance 'you must forgive'.

 (iii) Faith – as a mustard seed. – Say to this mulberry tree be uprooted – it will obey you.

 (iv) Servant – Servant waits on the master. – done his duty. – after doing the will of the master.

(2) Jesus heals 10 men with leprosy. —— RECOGNITION

   (i)   Place – along the border between Samaria and Galilee.

  (ii) Persons – ten leprous men.

 (iii) Plight – they call to Jesus "Jesus Master, have pity on us".

 (iv) Demands of the law – Go show yourselves to the priest.

  (v) One of them came back – Him fell at the feet of Jesus – and thanked Him – and he was a Samaritan.

(3) The coming kingdom of God. —— REALITY

(i) The kingdom of God is 'in you'.

(ii) The Son of Man – like lightening – Lighting the sky.

(iii) He must first 'suffer'.

(iv) As in the days of Noah. so in the day of – Two in a bed – Two women grinding corn.

(v) As in the days of Lot. the Son of Man – Two men in a field.

Whoever keeps his life will lose it, and whoever loses his life will keep it.

LUKE – CHAPTER 18

1. Parable of the persistent woman. – verses 1 – 8
2. Parable of the Pharisee and the tax collector. – verses 9 – 14
3. Children and Jesus. – verses 15 – 17
4. The rich and the kingdom of God – verses 18 –30
5. Jesus predicts His death – 3rd. time – verses 31 – 34
6. A blind beggar is healed – verses 35 – 43

(1) Parable of the persistent woman.
———— IMPORTUNITY

   (i) Lesson – men aught always to pray – not give up.

   (ii) Judge – feared not God – nor what people might say.

   (iii) There was a woman in the town that kept coming to him.

   (iv) Judge relents – finally gives in – settles the matter.

   (v) Persistency pays off – God will hear the cry of His people.

(2) Parable of the Pharisee and the tax collector.
———— IMPORTANCE

   (i) Self righteous – two men in the temple – Pharisee and tax collector.

   (ii) Pharisee prays about his good life. – Beggar prays God have mercy on me.

   (iii) Tax collector went down to his home 'justified'.

(3) Children and Jesus. ———————— INFANTS

    (i) The disciples rebuke those bringing children.

    (ii) But Jesus called the children to Him.

    (iii) Suffer the children – of such is the kingdom of God.

(4) The rich man and the kingdom of God. —— INVESTMENT

    (i) A certain ruler – "What must I do to inherit eternal life"?

    (ii) Why call Me good – none is good save God

    (iii) You know the commandments.

    (iv) All these things have I kept from my youth.

    (v) You still lack one thing.

    (vi) He loved his riches more than God – where is your love focussed.

    (vii) Upon this challenge – He went away – for he was very rich.

    (viii) Disciples ask – "Who then can be saved"?

    (ix) The things that are impossible with men are possible with God.

    (x) Loss in this life will be recompensed in the next life.

(5) Jesus predicts His death – 3rd Time. ———————— INFORMATION

    (i) Jesus takes aside His disciples.

    (ii) Tells them what is going to happen to Him.

    (iii) The disciples did not understand any of this.

(6) A blind beggar is healed. ——— IMPLORING

   (i) As Jesus approached Jericho – a blind man on the roadside.

  (ii) Asked the crowd who was passing.

 (iii) Told – Jesus of Nazareth.

 (iv) He called out "Jesus – Son of David" – Have mercy on me.

  (v) Jesus stopped – asked for him to be brought.

 (vi) "What do you want Me to do"?

(vii) "Lord – I want to see" was the reply.

(viii) Your faith has healed you.

LUKE – CHAPTER 19

1. Zacchaeus – the tax collector – verses 1 – 10
2. The parable of the 'ten minas'. – verses 11 – 27
3. Jesus comes to Jerusalem as King – verses 28 – 44
4. Jesus at the temple. – verses 45 – 48

(1) Zacchaeus – the tax collector. ——— SALVATION

    (i) Zacchaeus – chief tax collector – was wealthy.

    (ii) He wanted to see who Jesus was.

    (iii) He was short – so he climbed up a tree.

    (iv) When Jesus reached the spot He said "Zacchaeus come down".

    (v) At once – welcomed Him gladly.

    (vi) Some of the people muttered complained.

    (vii) Zacchaeus stood up and said.

    (viii) "Lord, I give half of my possessions to the poor."

    (ix) And if I have cheated anyone – I repay them four times as much.

    (x) Jesus said "Today is salvation come to this house."

(2) The parable of the 'ten minas' ——— SERVICE

    (i) The people had a misconception of the 'kingdom of God'.

    (ii) The parable was to remove that.

    (iii) The noblemen went away to receive a kingdom.

  (iv) He called his servants to see if they had put his money to work.

  (v) But they sent after him saying "we do not want this man as king".

(3) Jesus comes to Jerusalem as king. —— SALUTATION & SADNESS

  (i) Jesus approaches Bethpage and Bethany.

  (ii) Instructs 'His disciples concerning a colt'.

  (iii) The disciples found it as Jesus had said.

  (iv) They brought the colt to the Lord.

  (v) Jesus enters Jerusalem – the crowds 'Hail Him'.

  (vi) Some of the Pharisees tell Jesus to rebuke them.

  (vii) Jesus replies "If they keep quiet the very stones will cry out".

(4) Jesus at the temple. —— STRICTURE

  (i) Jesus enters the temple and drives out those engaged in selling.

  (ii) My house is a house of 'Prayer' – you have turned it into a den of thieves.

  (iii) The chief priests, teachers of the law, and leaders begin plotting to kill Him.

It was worship through convenience, profiteering on the basis of 'religious devotion', the religious leaders sanctioned this.

LUKE – CHAPTER 20

1. Jesus's authority questioned. _ verses 1 – 8
2. The parable of the tenants – verses 9 – 15
3. Paying taxes to Caesar – verses 16 – 26
4. The resurrection and Marriage. – verses 27 – 40
5. Whose son is Messiah – verses 41 – 44
6. Warning against teachers of the law. – verses 45 – 48

(1) Jesus's authority questioned. ⸻ DISSENT

    (i) Chief priests, teachers of the law & elders – By what authority are you doing these things.?

    (ii) Jesus replies "Tell Me", the baptism of John – is it of men or of God.

    (iii) We don't know where it is from.

    (iv) Neither do I *tell you by what authority I do these things.*

(2) The parable of the tenants. ⸻ DELIBERATION

    (i) A man planted a vineyard.

    (ii) Rented it to farmers – expecting fruit.

    (iii) But no fruit was forthcoming.

    (iv) Servant of the master sent – they beat him and sent him away.

    (v) 2nd & 3rd servants sent – same thing happened.

    (vi) Sent his Son – this is the Heir – let us kill him.

    (vii) Master will kill those farmers – Give the vineyard to others.

(viii) The stone which the builders rejected.

(ix) Leaders knew that the parable applied to them.

(3) Paying taxes to Caesar. —— DIRECTIVE
   (i) Leaders sent spies who appeared sincere.
   (ii) They hoped to catch Jesus in his words.
   (iii) Spies ask Jesus is it lawful to pay taxes to Caesar?
   (iv) Jesus replied "Show Me a denarius"
   (v) "Whose superscription is this" – Caesar's.
   (vi) Render to Caesar what is Caesar's and to God what is God's.

(4) The resurrection and marriage. —— DETAIL
   (i) Some of the Sadducees came to Jesus.
   (ii) A man and his brothers (seven) had to wife, on death, the same woman.
   (iii) In the resurrection whose wife will she be?
   (iv) Those worthy to take part in the resurrection neither marry nor are given in marriage – but are like the angels.
   (v) At the burning bush Moses showed 'the dead live', God is God of the living.

(5) Whose Son is Messiah? —— DAVID
   (i) They answer "David's Son".
   (ii) Why does David say "The Lord said unto MY Lord".
   (iii) David calls Him Lord, how then is He his son?
   (iv) Warnings given against 'Teachers of the Law'.
   (v) They are 'superficial' not keeping the law they teach.
   (vi) They will be severely punished.

(6) Warnings against teachers of the4 Law ——— DANGER

   (i)   Jesus warns His disciples of the teachers of the Law.

   (ii)   They are superficial not keeping the law they teach.

   (iii) They will be severely punished.

LUKE – CHAPTER 21

1. The widow's offering. – verse 1 – 4
2. The destruction of the temple – verses 5 – 37

(1) The widow's offering. —— DONATIONS

    (i)   Sincerity in giving is taken account of by God.

    (ii) Jesus saw the rich putting in their gifts – the temple offering.

    (iii) He also saw the poor widow put in two coins.

    (iv) She has put in more than they all.

    (v) The rich put in of their ABUNDANCE – but she out of her poverty.

(see 2 Corinthians ch. 9 verse 12)

(2) The destruction of the temple – end times. —— DESCRIPTION

    (i) Whilst he disciples were admiring the temple structure and gifts.

    (ii) Jesus revealed to them its destruction.

    (iii) They ask the Lord "When shall these things be"?

    (iv) Jesus replied "Watch out for DECEIVERS".

    (v) There will be wars, rumours of wars, earthquakes, famines, kingdom against kingdom, fearful events, great signs in the heavens.

    (vi) The end will not come right away.

    (vii) There will be persecution and harassment.

(viii) When you bear testimony to my name. When you see Jerusalem being surrounded.

(ix) I will give you words and wisdom.

(x) Everyone will hate you because of Me.

(xi) When you see Jerusalem being surrounded.

(xii) Know that the end is near (see Revelation ch. 20 v 9)

(xiii) How dreadful it will be 'in those days'.

(xiv) There will be signs in the sun, moon and stars.

(xv) People will faint from terror at what is coming on the world.

(xvi) At that time they will see the Son of Man coming.

(xvii) Lift up your heads – Your redemption draws nigh.

(xviii) The fig tree and all the trees sprout – the kingdom of God is near.

LUKE – CHAPTER 22

(1) Judas agrees to betray Jesus
(2) The last supper
(3) Jesus prays on the mount
(4) Jesus is arrested
(5) Peter disowns Jesus
(6) The guards mock Jesus
(7) Jesus before Pilate and Herod

(1) Judas agrees to betray Jesus. —— DECEIT

    (i) Chief priests and elders look for a way to get rid of Jesus.

    (ii) Then Satan enters Judas.

    (iii) They discuss with Judas a plan.

(2) The last supper. —— DESIRE

    (i) Day of unleavened bread – Passover lamb sacrificed.

    (ii) Jesus sends Peter & John to prepare a place.

    (iii) They enter the city, see a man, ask "Where is the room"?

    (iv) "He will show you a large upper room"

    (v) Make preparations there.

    (vi) Jesus gathers with His own.

    (vii) The bread, the wine, not partake again until the Kingdom of God.

    (viii) The hand of the betrayer is with Me on the table.

    (ix) Features of the children of the Kingdom.

  (x) Reward for Loyalty conferred on them a kingdom.

  (xi) Satan's request re. Simon Peter.

  (xii) The Lord's prediction concerning Peter.

  (xiii) The fulfilment approaches – Swords prepared.

(3) Jesus prays n the Mount of Olives. —— DEVOTION

  (i)   Jesus went to the mount with His disciples.

  (ii)   Jesus exhorts them to pray.

  (iii) Jesus withdraws himself to pray.

  (iv) Jesus returns to find them sleeping.

  (v)   Exhorts them to get up and pray.

(4) Jesus is arrested. —— DEMONIC

  (i)   While He was speaking Judas comes with the crowd.

  (ii)   Jesus asks him "Do you betray with a kiss"?

  (iii) Jesus healsthe ear – instructs His own – No more of this.

  (iv) Jesus asks His enemies "Why do you come with arms to take Him"?

(5) Peter disowns Jesus. —— DENIAL

  (i)   Peter followed at a distance and sat down 'with them'.

  (ii)   The servant girl accuses him – He denies.

  (iii) Later a man recognised him – He denies.

  (iv) Then another asserts – He denies.

  (v)   Immediately the cock crew – He went out and wept bitterly.

(6) The guards mock Jesus. —— DERISION

(i) The men who were guarding Jesus – mocked Him.

(ii) Then started to insult Him.

(7) Jesus before Pilate and Herod

(i) Councils of the chief priests, elders and teachers of the law meet together to 'Judge Jesus'

(ii) They ordered Him "Tell us if you are the Messiah"

(iii) Jesus answered "If I tell you – you will not believe"

(iv) "From now on the Son of Man will be seated at Mighty God's right hand"

(v) They all asked "are you the Son of God"?

LUKE – CHAPTER 23

(1) Jesus led to Pilate
(2) The crucifixion of Jesus
(3) The death of Jesus
(4) The burial of Jesus

(1) Jesus led to Pilate. ——— TRIAL

   (i) The whole assembly rose up and 'led Him to Pilate' They asked for the release of Barrabus

   (ii) Pilate asked Jesus "Are you the king of the Jews"?

   (iii) "You have said so" Began in Galilee

   (iv) When Pilate heard this he sent Him to Herod satisfy his curiosity.

   (vi) But Jesus did not accommodate him.

   (vi) Herod and his soldiers ridiculed and mocked Him.

   (vii) Jesus was returned to Pilate – He would punish and release Him.

   (viii) But the whole crowd cried "Away with this man"

   (ix) They asked for Barrabus to be released.

   (x) They kept shouting "Crucify, Crucify"

   (xi) For the third time Pilate says "I find no fault in Him"

   (xii) Upon their constant shouting Pilate gave in.

   (xiii) Pilate delivered Jesus to their will.

(2) The crucifixion of Jesus. —— TAUNTING

   (i) The soldiers led Him away.

   (ii) They laid hold of Simon of Cyrene to carry 'His cross'

   (iii) Jesus says to the daughters of Jerusalem "weep not for me"

   (iv) Weep for your children – Judgement is soon to come.

   (v) Two other men (criminals) were led out with Him.

   (vi) When they were come to the 'place' they 'crucified Him'

   (vii) One of the criminals said "aren't you the Messiah"? – save yourself and us.

   (viii) The other said "Lord remember me"

   (ix) Jesus replied "Today you will be with Me in paradise"

(3) The death of Jesus. —— TERMINATION

   (i) About noon the sun was darkened.

   (ii) The curtain of the temple was torn in two.

   (iii) Jesus cried "Father into your hands I commend My spirit."

   (iv) And He breathed His last.

   (v) The centurion worshipped God.

   (vi) The women 'stood at a distance' watching.

(4) The burial of Jesus. —— TOMB

(i)   A man named Joseph.

(ii)   Good and upright – had not consented to their actions.

(iii)   Was waiting for the Kingdom of God.

(iv)   Went to Pilate and begged the body of Jesus.

(v)   Placed it in the tomb.

(vi)   The disciples went home – because it was the Sabbath.

LUKE – CHAPTER 24

(1) Jesus is risen' ——— RESURRECTION

    (i)   On the first day – women took spices.

    (ii)   They went to the tomb – found the stone rolled away.

    (iii)   Angels appeared – "why do you seek the living among the dead"?

    (iv)   He is not here – He is risen.

    (v)   They went and told the disciples all these things (ie. the eleven)

    (vi)   The disciples did not believe them.

    (vii)   Peter ran to the tomb and found it so.

(2) On the road to Emmaus. ——— RECOGNITION

    (i)   Now that same day – Two going to Emmaus.

    (ii)   While they conversed – Jesus drew near.

    (iii)   They did not recognise Him.

    (iv)   He asked details of their conversation.

    (v)   Cleophas said "Are you the only one, visiting Jerusalem, and do not know."?

(vi) "What things"? asked the Saviour – concerning Jesus of Nazareth.

(vii) "How foolish you are" ———.

(viii) Slow to believe – Moses and the prophets – all that they have spoken.

(ix) They reached the village and urged Jesus to join them.

(xi) At the table during breaking of bread they recognised Him.

(xii) Did not our hearts burn within us as He opened the scriptures.

(xiii) They returned to Jerusalem to tell the eleven.

(xiv) It is true – the Lord is risen 'indeed'.

(3) Jesus appears to His disciples. ——— REVELATION

  (i) As they conversed together, Jesus appeared 'in their midst'

  (ii) Saying to them "Peace be unto you".

  (iii) He showed them His hands and His feet.

  (iv) And then ate a piece of broiled fish.

  (v) This is what I told you.

  (vi) Then He opened their minds.

  (vii) "You are the witnesses of these things."

  (viii) "I am sending you clothed with POWER"

(4) Jesus's ascension ——— RISING

  (i) He led them as far as Behtany.

  (ii) Lifted up His hands and blessed them.

  (iii) Was taken up from them.

  (iv) They returned to Jerusalem

CHARACTERS IN THE GOSPEL OF JOHN

CHAPTER 1

NATHANAEL

In this wondrous event described in the writings of his day and of which, while under the fig tree, he was turning over in his mind and longing to see it, in his day; this great event that would usher in all the dreams of the nation and bring release from the bondage of Rome and blessing to the nation.

We have found Him was the declaration of Philip, as he with great enthusiasm revealed the stupendous news to his fellow Israelite.

The next declaration was to cause immediate doubt and frustration as Philip stated 'Jesus of Nazareth the son of Joseph'. The possibility exists that Nathanael thought 'no, not again' yet another unsubstantiated claim, falsely made, to attract attention, but just another 'son' born to an ordinary carpenter, called Joseph, of no real breeding and coming from a despised area in Israel, of gentile habitation, with little or no importance in the larger scheme of things.

"Can there good thing come out of Nazareth"? was the rebuff that Philip received from an individual who knew many of the writings of his day and was influenced by them in his thinking.

William Kelly writes in his commentary 'had Philip said from Bethlehem – the Son of David no such shock would have been given to an expectant Jew', but Nazareth, and the son of Joseph could not be accepted and was thus rejected.

The response of Philip was directed by God's Spirit – 'come and see'. No debate, no argument, no declaration of resentment, but a simple reply 'come and see' for yourself. These words were spoken by the Saviour himself when asked by the two disciples "where do you dwell"? his reply was 'come and see'.

This invitation is relevant today, as the Saviour says to all who would listen and respond "come and see", but so often it is refused by so many who choose to reject such a gracious offer, which could change their lives with untold blessings and eternal security.

Despite Nathanael's assessment of the good news relayed by Philip, the Saviour on meeting Nathanael, saw a man with an indestructible desire for the realisation of God's kingdom and a character which conveyed 'no deceit' (guile), a true Israelite. This revelation by the Saviour impacted the heart and mind of Nathanael, so much so, that he asks the question of the Lord

"Since when do you know me"? Another revelation followed when the Saviour declared "When you were under the fig tree, I saw you". This revelation was sufficient to convince Nathanael that someone special was before him. Before Philip even called him, when he was beneath the fig tree, possibly with thoughts of the kingdom, for which he longed, – since the fig tree would have been a reminder of the nation of Israel and its fruit, which was not evident in that day of subjugation to Rome and thus the hope of the kingdom was far removed.

Such thoughts were already known to the Saviour, hence the Saviour declares "because I saw you under the fig tree you believe, you shall see greater things than these, you shall see heaven opened and the angels of God ascending and descending upon the Son of Man".

What a revelation Nathanael received on this encounter with the Saviour such that he made confession straightway "Rabbi, you are the Son of God, you are the King of Israel" No longer the son of Joseph, no longer the despised Nazarene, but the Son of God and the King of Israel.

At last the dream is realised, the King has come, Messiah has arrived, the kingdom is sure.

'Hallelujah'

Many there are, like Nathanael, of fixed opinion and inflexible, until an encounter with the Saviour, and truth is revealed, so that fixed, even traditional beliefs are removed and the truth makes us 'free', salvation is experienced and real hope replaces false expectations.

CHAPTER 2

INDIVIDUAL – NICODEMAS – JOHN CHAPTER 3 VERSES 1 – 21 – THE MAN OF SEARCH-ING SPIRIT AND PERCEPTION

John tells us there was a man of the Pharisees named Nicodemus, a ruler of the Jews.

A man – one of the human race.

A Pharisee – one some standing.

A ruler – a Teacher of the Jews.

His identity, his religious beliefs and his position in the community is all revealed in one fiell swoop.

A man named 'Nicodemus'; we ar left in no doubt as to his identity. God always deals with individuals where such is desirous of seeking the 'truth' and so it is with this man named Nicodemas. IGod not only knows us by name but the very hairs of our head are numbered by Him. (see Luke ch. 12 v 7) such is God's knowledge of our being. There is nothing that is hid from His eyes. (see Hebrews ch. 4 verse 13)

A Pharisee, of particular religious persuasion. a sect of Jewish origin generally known as 'pious ones'. Josephus says of them 'supreme sanctity of life', devotion to God and their study of the law. Such was Nicodemus, but something was missing in his life, hence is going to the Saviour, albeit by night, to get to understand the patent and obvious evidence of miracle working and the conclusion that 'God must be with Him' (see ch. 3 verse 2)

The Saviour does not hesitate to answer him and declare the fact of 'new birth' as the secret to entry into the kingdom of God viz. 'except a man be born again he cannot see the kingdom of God' Such a declaration was foreign to the mind of Nicodemus (though a Teacher of Israel) He had not heard this before and was clearly bemused by such a revelation. His response was one of complete ignorance, as indicated by his reply to the Lord, "How can a man be born when he is old"? Nicodemus is unable to rise above the physical in his thinking, so the Saviour explains by declaring it is birth by the water and the Spirit. The water referred to is the Word of God, and the Spirit is the Holy Ghost who applies the Word to the soul to bring about 'the new birth'. The lesson is reinforced by the words of the Lord "That which is born of the flesh is flesh and that which is born of the Spirit is spirit"; marvel not that I said to you "You must be born again" The two are separate, the physical and the spiritual, and operate in separate realms.

Nicodemus is still perplexed and states "How can these things be"? The Saviour answers "are you a teacher in Israel and you don't know these things"? "If I have told you of earthly things and you do not believe, how shall you believe if I tell you of heavenly things"? The Saviour has revealed new teaching to the teacher. He now proceeds to instruct him regarding that which is familiar to Nicodemus, even the story of Moses lifting up the serpent in the wilderness. It now becomes clear what the real application of the event signifies. As Moses lifted up the serpent in the wilderness even so must the Son of Man be lifted up (upon a cross) that whosoever believes in Him should not perish but have eternal life.

We then have the greatest verse in all scripture uttered by the Saviour "For God so loved the world that He gave His only begotten Son that whosoever believes in Him should not perish but have everlasting life (John ch. 3 verse 16).

What a revelation to Nicodemus, that God should send His own Son into the world, not to condemn the world but to save the world. The condemnation was already there (see John ch. 3 v 19) that men loved darkness rather than light. Those seeking and doing the truth come to the light that their deeds may be manifest and wrought in God. Such was the case with Nicodemus a man of seeking spirit who had come to the Light and had his needs met by the man of Nazareth even the Son of God, the Messiah. Is that your position dear soul. Do you seek the truth like Nicodemus, are you willing to meet with the Saviour and listen to His word.?

Have you experienced the impact of those searching words 'You must be born again'?

Marvel not that the Saviour, Jesus Christ, the Son of God said "You must be born again".

Individual – Woman of Samaria – John chapter 4 verses 5 – 30.

A woman of questionable morals but aware of her surroundings and culture.

The introduction to this encounter is challenging to say the least. Jesus left Judaea to go into 'Galilee' because He 'must needs go through Samaria' and reach Sychar, near to a parcel of ground that Jacob gave to his son Joseph containing Jacob's well. Though leaving Judah He was still to carry with it the history of a past day of blessing to Israel's patriarch Jacob and his son Joseph as a foundation for an oncoming converse with a Samaritan woman (see chapter 4 verse9)

The contact was now made (chapter 4 verse 7) 'there came a woman of Samaria and Jesus asked for a drink. Two traditions are now brought forward, one' how is it that you being a Jew asks a drink of me – for the jews have no dealings with the Samaritans. Two, which am a woman of Samaria (see verse 27) and His disciples marvelled that He conversed with a woman

There now follows a more amazing declaration from the Saviour. If you knew the gift of God and who it is that asks drink the positions would be reversed and you would be asking of Him because He could give you 'living water'.

Like Nicodemus in chapter 3 the woman dwelt on the 'physical'

You have nothing to draw with – the well is deep – Are you greater than Jacob who gave us this well?

The Lord now moves her to the spiritual realm saying "whoever drinks of this water will thirst again" Whoever drinks of the water that I shall give him shall never thirst, but will have a well of water springing up into ' everlasting life'. The response of the woman is still on a physical level. She says 'Sir give me this water' (i) so that I thirst not (ii)   that I do not have to come to this well and draw.

The point has now been reached in the conversation to deal with her personal life and to tell her to go and fetch her husband upon which she declares "I have no husband". The Saviour then reveals that she has had five husbands and her present husband is not her husband in this you speak the truth, taken by surprise by the revelation by the Lord then she asks "whence do you know me"? (see chapter 1 verse 48). Such knowledge is beyond human ingenuity, so the woman declares" Sir I perceive that you are a prophet"

The woman now moves to the spiritual and declares what she has known for sometime in her life; the tradition of the fathers and where they worshipped ie. in that mountain and not at Jerusalem. The Saviour now reveals, not where worship is to be entered into, but how worship must be executed and on what grounds for salvation is from the Jews, and 'true worship' must be executed in Spirit and in Truth for the Father seeks such to worship Him.

At this point we have the final revelation given in answer to the woman's declaration "When Messiah comes He will explain everything" (verse 25). Jesus states "I that speak to you am He (the Messiah). The woman then left her water pot and went into the town declaring" Come see a man that told all things that ever I did is not this the Christ? They then went out to see and came to Him and many of the Samaritans 'believed on Him'. They said tom the woman. Now we believe not because of what you said, we have heard ourselves and we know that this man really is the Saviour of the world.

Individual – unnamed – the noblemen of Capernaum – John chapter 4 verse 46 – 54.

A man who was a royal officer but came to Jesus for help.

This individual is not named but was desperate to see Jesus that He might heal his son who was at the point of death. He was a man of some position, but John tells us that he literally 'begged' Jesus to come and heal his son.

The reply of the Saviour was calculated to induce a response which would demonstrate this man's genuineness and his willingness to believe the words of the Lord. Jesus said to him "Except you see signs and wonders, you will not believe". The man says again "Sir come down before my child dies". The challenge is now issued as then Lord says "Go your way, your son lives". Remarkably the man 'believed' the word that Jesus had spoken and went his way.

What belief and trust this man exercised recognising the authority of the Saviour and His power to heal. Now as he was going down his servants met him and told him "your son lives" Much elation would naturally have followed the good news, but the nobleman was more interested in the hour when the son began to get better (recover) and they told him 'yesterday at the 7th hour the fever left him'. Then the man knew that it was the same hour in which Jesus said "your son lives".

There are three major lessons to be learned as a testimony from this event verse 12;

(1) The power of Jesus to transform a situation is irrefutable.
(2) The word of Jesus to effect a change in life's experience is absolutely reliable.

(3) The timing of such is precise and apt.

So the father knew that it was at the 'same hour' in which Jesus said 'your son lives' and he believed and his whole house.

Experience is something that convinces the individual of the reality of an event or fact that has taken place in which he or she has been involved or witnessed. Such is the case here, where the nobleman had not only been involved but had also witnessed the power of Jesus, the word of Jesus and the timing of Jesus.

Distance made no difference to the outcome, the actual presence of the Saviour in the house when the son was ill was not necessary, and the precise timing of the act of healing was of real import in the situation. John tells us this is the second miracle Jesus did in Galilee as a testimony to the Galileans of the power and word of Christ as God's Messiah.

Once again we see the mercy of God in the lies of individuals to teach us that God is the God of the individual as individual is in need of salvation, deliverance from death, not physical. but eternal. The soul has an eternal existence and a such requires saving from an existence inn separation from God, hence the words of the Saviour "What shall it profit a man if he gain the whole world and 'lose' his own soul. or what shall a man give in exchange for his soul" (see Matthew chapter 16 verses 25 – 26).

Individual – A lad here – John chapter 6 verses 9 – 18.

A lad of curious intellect – but willing spirit.

What a day of revelation and surprise for a boy curious to find out about this remarkable man from Nazareth of whom so much had been said and so much had been witnessed concerning His miraculous power. It would appear he was with a large company, unaccompanied, but with sufficient food to see him through the day. He must also have been near to the Lord and disciples for Andrew to notice what he carried.

There is a lad here is all we know about this young man in terms of his identity, but much is revealed about his character in what follows.

   (i)   He was in the right place

   (ii)   He was there at the right time

   (iii) He was the source of a great miracle to follow – right source

   (iv)   He was willing to yield to the Saviour – who would take his lunch

   (v)   He witnessed first hand, the great power of the Saviour

   (vi)   What a story he had to tell back home with five barley loaves and two fish

   (i)   You cannot say that this was planned by the action of the disciples. (There is a lad here) indicates that the lad happened to be in an appropriate place (though known to the Lord) so as to be available with just five loaves and two fishes

   (ii)   The time was also apt since the Lord had posed the question 'Whence shall we buy bread for these people to eat."? There is a lad here (right now) with five barley loaves and two small fish, already to hand.

(iii)   A source so small and insufficient for such a crowd, yet in then Saviour's hands enough to meet the need of so great a multitude in want.

(iv)   The release of this lad's lunch was indicative of the right attitude hr showed, being willing to let the Saviour do what He would with the seemingly paltry offering – he would see what the 'touch of the master's hand would produce'.

(v)   What a wonderful experience was to be given to this lad as he witnessed the power of the Saviour to feed over five thousand plus people from just five loaves and two fish.

He had seen, first hand, what he had possibly heard and which had given rise to his desire to see this man from Nazareth who possessed such miraculous power.

(vi)   What a story he had to tell on his return to his home. A privileged onlooker to the fantastic miracle executed by this man, called the Messiah and thus was able to perform such miracles.

Are you, dear reader, ready and willing to believe, like this young lad, to hand over your life, as an offering, so that the 'touch of the masters hand' can transform your life to make something of infinite worth both to yourself and your fellow man, and dispense blessings in their world, to humankind, so needy in their traverse through life.

CHAPTER 7

WOMAN TAKEN IN ADULTERY – JOHN CHAPTER 8 VERSES 3 – 11

Individual – unnamed – A woman of moral indiscretion, found guilty but forgiven

Once again the Scribes and the Pharisees seek to challenge the Saviour as to His authority and teaching, taking this woman and bringing her before Him, she having been caught in the very act of adultery. They quote the words of Moses and the law and issue the challenge to the Lord by saying "What do you say"? hoping to tempt and accuse the Lord.

Would He contradict the words of Moses and thus be a law breaker, such was the objective of this company as they challenged Him with, what they considered to be cast iron closed case. The Saviour seemed to ignore their words and stooped down to write in the ground. Much has been speculated as to what He wrote, the scripture is silent, but the continual asking of the Scribes and Pharisees caused the Lord to lift himself up and reply to their challenge. The word He spoke was to cause an impact that could not be expected "He that is without sin among you let him first cast a stone at her", and again He stooped down and wrote on the ground.

What a challenge this was for them, who would dare to say "I am without sin" not one of them, out of conviction by their own conscience, and were forced to depart one by one from the eldest to the last. The scene has now changed and Jesus is left alone, for He saw none but the woman who had been in the midst of the commotion. The Saviour now addresses her and says "Woman where are your accusers, has no one condemned you"? "No one Lord" was the reply; "Neither do I condemn you, go and sin no more".

Who would have believed such a thing could happen? The law demanded death by stoning, but grace brought forgiveness. Hallelujah!!! The wages of sin is death, but the gift of God is eternal life through Jesus Christ our Lord. (see Romans chapter 6 verse 27).

How many souls, like this particular woman, are caught and brought to face the result of their sinful, acts and are condemned by society, land in prison, and have a future stained with the shame of their sinful acts. Condemnation is easily resorted to, but to give encouragement and purpose to such is not easy. The Saviour is the master of such situations and offers the individual hope, purpose and rest. His promise is true and totally reliable as He says "come unto me and I will give you rest, take my yoke upon you and learn of me, for I am meek and lowly in heart ad you shall find rest to your soul". (see Matthew ch. 11 verse 29)

Individual – unnamed – A man willing to obey and testify – John ch. 9 v's 1 – 38

The focus of this miracle is to demonstrate the obedience that of both the Saviour (ch. 9 v 41) and the man born blind (ch. 9 v 7). The power of the Saviour to heal and the unquestioning obedience of the man born "blind are words (ch. 9 v 5) which the Pharisees, in their envy and hatred, refused to accept (ch. 9 v 16)" again questioning the breaking of the Sabbath.

What follows is a dissection of what took place and how the man received his sight. The first inquired were the neighbours who had known the blind man from his birth and wanted to know how he was made to see some said it is him, others said he is like him, but he said 'I am him'. Testimony of *God's saving grace begins with telling family and friends and neighbours of* the miracle of God's working to change the life of the individual, The man born blind had a tremendous change in his life, a change that could not be hidden, thus in answer to the enquiry (ch. 9 v 10) he answered "A man called Jesus" such words, spoken with authority and conviction when accepted and obeyed yield such blessings as to be almost unbelievable.

They, presumably the neighbours, bring the man to the Pharisees who now engage in an investigation as to how he had received his sight (ch. 9 v 15). The testimony of the man born blond is direct and to the point, no fanciful description, but straightforward, plain, and easy to understand ~ He put clay on my eyes and I washed and do see "He does not mention on the Sabbath or an ritual or tradition but simply what took place, immediately the Pharisees resort to the law and tradition and a division arises among them". The Pharisees now ask the man "What do you say about your eyes being opened by Hm"? he replies "He is a prophet"

There is a way out of this dilemma was the response of the Jewish religious leaders by stating he was not born blind so they send for his parents.

The testimony of the parents is solid and irrefutable "We know that this is our son and that he was born blind" A salutary lesson is to be learned here from the physical situation translated into the spiritual realm 'We are often told the all are the children of God, of whatever race or creed as to identity but not so often is it proclaimed that all are born blind in a spiritual sense as knowledge of God through 'new birth' (see John ch. 3) is not acknowledged as a requisite for entry into the kingdom of God.

Confession of Jesus as the Christ meant expulsion from the synagogue so the parents reverted to making the son responsible by saying "he is of age ask him, he shall speak for himself" the challenge was now directed towards the son who stood his ground in terms of the truth of what took place unique experience "whether he be a sinner or not I know not, one thing I know whereas once I was blind now I see".

You cannot take away a persons experience!!! Their persistence is immovable the man born blind answered "I have already told you and you did not listen, will you also be His disciples"? The pharisees then reviled him accusing him of preaching as one of Christ's disciples. The rebuff given by the once blind man is cutting as he debated with them the pros and cons of the situation stating" why herein is a 'marvellous thing' from where He is yet He has opened my eyes. Now we know this who does God's will 'Him He hears'. If this man were not of 'God He could do nothing'. on this they cast him out.

Jesus heard that they had cast him out and found him, He then asked him "Do you believe in the Son of God. The answer the once blind man gives is "who is he Lord that I might believe"? The lord replies "you have seen Him and it is He that talks with you". The once blind man replies "Lord I believe" and he worshipped Him What a conclusion the blind see whilst those who claim to see remain blind (ch. 9 verse 34). Dear one as you are, in the position of seeing physically though once blind spiritually, or do you still, in rejection of the word of the Saviour, remain blinded by other voices declaring their refusal of God's revelation in Christ.

CHAPTER 10

INDIVIDUAL – LAZARUS – JOHN CHAPTER 11 VERSES 1 – 44

A man loved by Jesus, but sick in body, and raised by Jesus from the dead

John now introduces us to a family, two sisters and a brother, with whom Jesus had formed a close relationship and spent many an hour in their presence, at their home, in Bethany, so much so that John records (ch. 11 v 5) 'Now Jesus loved Martha and her sister and Lazarus.'

News reaches Jesus of the sickness of Lazarus and declares that the 'sickness' was not unto death but for the glory of God, and upon that declaration Jesus remained two days in the place where He was. If, as was stated, Jesus loved Lazarus, you would have thought He would hasten to Bethany to see him and perchance heal him. Not so; when walking in the will of God, the individual acts often contrary to what man reasons in the situation and is confident of the outcome, because his trust is in God.

Jesus now addresses His disciples and tells them "our friend Lazarus sleeps, but I go to awake him out of sleep". His disciples fail to grasp the implication of the words of the Saviour so He has to tell them plainly "Lazarus is dead" and adds the words "let us go to him". Thomas says to the other disciples "let us go with Him". A large company had gathered to comfort Martha and Mary concerning their brother, but Martha had heard that Jesus was coming ad wet to meet Him, greeting Him with the words "Lord if you had been here my brother would not have died, but even now whatever you will ask of God, God will give it you".

Jesus said to her "your brother will rise again", she replied "I know that he shall rise again in the resurrection at the last day" Jesus answered "I am the resurrection and the life; he that believes in me though he were dead yet shall he live, and whoever lives and believes in Me shall never die – do you believe this"? Marhta replies "yes Lord I believe that you are the Christ, the Son of God which should come into the word".

Martha then went to call Mary saying "the Master is come and is calling for you", Mary rises and upon reaching Jesus she repeats the words of Martha saying "Lord if you had been here my brother would not have died", but does not go further as did Martha, but fell at His feet weeping. Death to so many seems so final, and even the Lord. when reaching the tomb of Lazarus 'wept' for He knew the ravages of death, and the reason it had entered the world, also the reason why He had come into the world, ie to remove the pain of death by His own death bringing a note of victory over death (see 1 Corinthians ch. 15 v 54).

The Jews questioned His power "Could this man, which opened the eyes of the blind, that even this man should not have died"? The demonstration of the power of the Lord is quite dramatic; standing before the grave He says "Take away the stone" Martha protests saying "Lord by this time he stinks for he has been dead four days" The reply of the Lord was to say "Did not I tell you if you believe you shall see the glory of God". They took away the stone, and after praying and giving thanks, He cried with a loud voice "Lazarus come forth" and he that was dead came forth, bound hand and foot. Jesus commanded "loose him and let him go".

What the Jews witnessed was beyond belief and believed on Him, but others went their way to tell the Pharisees what things Jesus had done!! While the Pharisees took counsel against Jesus one of them, named Caiaphas declared that it was expedient that 'one man' should die for the nation, rather than the whole nation perish, but from that day forward they took counsel to kill Him. Jesus therefore walked no more openly among the Jews.

The feast of Passover was imminent and the religious rulers had given commandment if any knew of the whereabouts of Jesus they should show it that they might take Him. In the face of such a miracle and undeniable evidence of God's power being manifested by Jesus they remained unmoved and even to the extent of destroying their Messiah, sent from God. Many today epitomise the same spirit when it comes to acknowledging who Jesus is and what His teaching demands, in regard to the saving of the soul by the means that God has provided.

Individual – Pilate – A man lacking conviction – given to compromise – John ch's 18 & 19

Having examined Jesus before Caiaphas, the high priest, who asked Jesus about His disciples and His doctrine to which the Lord replied "Why do you ask me, ask them which heard me, they know what I said and in secret have I said nothing"? Then they led Jesus from Caiaphas to the hall of judgement where Pilate resides.

Pilate went out to them and said "What accusation do you bring against this man"? In answer they said "if he was not a malefactor, we would not have brought Him to you". Pilate answered "you take Him and judge Him according to your law" and their answer was "it is not lawful for us to put any man to death". At this point Pilate took responsibility to execute judgement by examining Jesus. The first question asked by Pilate was "Are you the King of the Jews"? Jesus answered "is this thing coming from your own reasoning or did someone else tell you"? Pilate replied, your own people delivered you to me "what have you done"? Jesus answered "My kingdom is not of this world".

Pilate then asked "Are you a King then"? The Saviour declared "to this end I was born and for this cause came I into the world, everyone who hears my voice hears the truth". Pilate replies "What is truth"? Upon this Pilate went out again to the people (Jews) and said "I find no fault in Him, but you have a custom that I should release to you one at the Passover, will you therefore I release to you 'the King of the Jews', they cried altogether" not this man but Barrabus, now Barrabus was a robber.

Prior to this Pilate had received a message from his wife saying "have nothing to do with this just man for I have suffered many things in a dream this day because of Him (see Matthew ch. 27 v's 19 – 26) Matthew in his account of the proceedings records that Pilate asked "Which of the two will you have me release to you"? The Jews cried out "Barrabus" "What then shall l do with Jesus which is called Christ. they all cried "Let Him be crucified". Pilate asks yet again "Why, what evil has He done"? but they became more determined saying "Let Him be crucified"

When Pilate could see that he could prevail nothing, he took water and washed his hands before the multitude saying "I am innocent of the blood of this just person, you see to it" and all the people answered "his blood be upon us and upon our children" and Pilate delivered Jesus, after scourging Him, to be crucified. Pilate had reckoned that he had a way out of the situation when he heard that Jesus came from Galilee and asked if Jesus was a Galilean. As soon as he knew that Jesus was belonging to Herod's jurisdiction he sent Jesus to Herod who was at Jerusalem at that time.

Herod was extremely glad to see Jesus for he wanted Jesus to perform a miracle for him but the Saviour answered him nothing and Herod, with his men of war, set Jesus at nought an d sent him to Pilate. Pilate again to the Jews (ie the chief priests and rulers) telling them that he and Herod found no cause of death to be done to Jesus and therefore to chastise Him and let Him go. But the crowd cried "Not this man but Barrabus" so determined were they to get rid of Jesus. Pilate lacked the courage to stand up to the religious leaders of the day and let them have their desire He was subsequently summoned to Rome to answer charges before the Emperor. He was banished and finally ended his life by his own hand,

Once again, like Judas Iscariot, he was privileged to have contact with the Saviour, to hear his words of truth, and have opportunity to act wisely, but chose not to do so, but to cede to the desires of men, in their hatred of God and to count the praise and wisdom of men more important than the praise and wisdom of God.

CHAPTER 11

MARY OF BETHANY –
JOHN CHAPTER 11
VERSES 1 – 11

Individual – A woman who worshipped the Lord by her actions and demonstrated her devotion to Him.

Mary's act of devotion to the Lord by anointing Him, whom she worshipped, was one of the great sacrifices of a follower of the Lord. Though condemned by those who witnessed the act, she is commended by the Saviour for the insight she exhibited in carrying out this anointing.

The words of the Saviour silenced those who were condemning this 'so called waste' of this precious commodity saying 'it could have sold for 300 pence and the yield given to the poor, which, on the surface, seemed a more profitable option and certainly appealed to the secular mind. Mary had the in sight to understand what lay before the Saviour, ie His impending death, and was prepared to sacrifice this costly ointment to His anointing and had kept it, so says the Saviour, against the day of His burying. Looks and mutterings of disapproval were all around and only one in the company spoke in approval of the act, the Lord himself.

It would appear that Mary had broken the container and poured all the contents over the Saviour, from head to feet, (see accounts in Matthew ch. 26 & Mark ch. 14), and then wiped His feet with her hair, the whole house being filled with the odour of the ointment. Mark tells us that the Saviour praised Mary for the 'good work' she had wrought on Him, as does Matthew, a double testimony approved and accepted and they, as gospel writers, add the words 'Wherever this gospel is preached in the whole world, there shall also this, that the woman has done be told for a memorial of her. (this double reference being significant since 'two' in scripture is the number of testimony.

This act of devotion to the Saviour would have an impact that was to be 'far reaching' and is set against the record of scripture concerning a completely opposite act of betrayal by Judas, for says Mathew and Mark in their account of the event of the memorable day, that Judas 'one of the twelve' went to the chief priests with a view to betraying the Lord. Thus we have on record two very distinct and opposite attitudes as to the person of Christ, one of absolute devotion led of God, and receiving divine approval, and the other, led of Satan and receiving divine retribution. 'Woe to that man who betrays the Son of Man (see Matthew ch. 26 verse 24) it had been good for that man had he had not been born'. (see Matthew ch. 26 verse 24)

Mary was well aware of the act she was undertaking, she was aware of the desire of the Lord's enemies to plot His death, hence the words of the Saviour "against the day of my burial has she kept this", thus the record of Matthew and Mark are in complete harmony with this.

Mary owed so much to the Saviour, the restoration of her brother from death, the salvation of her soul, and her identity with Him as the Messiah of God, so she would take opportunity to anoint Him as it presented itself in anticipation of His burial.

Mary's choice was of divine operation, whilst that of Judas was Satanic influence. The choosing of an action in regard to the Saviour is, for the individual, the same and critical since eternal destiny is at stake.

CHAPTER 12

INDIVIDUAL – SIMON PETER – JOHN CHAPTERS 12, 13, 18, 20 & 21

The man who spoke his mind but who sincerely loved the Lord

Our first introduction to Peter in John's gospel (ch. 1 v 42) is when Andrew brought him to Jesus and the Lord gave him the name Cephas (a stone). Peter the impetuous, forthright, impulsive individual who often spoke what he thought in an immediate response to the situation, sometimes with divine revelation and at other times inadvisably.

John records for us several events between Peter and the Saviour in which Peter is challenged by the Lord and learns to accede to the word of the Lord. Such is the situation in chapter 13 of John's gospel where the Saviour washes the feet of the disciples. John tells us 'then He comes to Simon Peter' and Peter responds with the words "Lord do you wash my feet"? In answer to the question the Lord gives the reply, "What I do now you know not but you shall know hereafter" Peter answers "you will never wash my feet" to which the Saviour replies "If I do not wash you, you have no part with me".

Peter knew little of the humiliation through which the Lord must pass in the path to the cross; far greater humiliation than that of washing the feet of the disciples which is what Peter saw at this time and, speaking on a human level said "You shall never wash my feet".

The use of the word 'part' in the Saviour's response can be better translated 'share' which was to be Peter's experience very shortly as the Saviour would be taken by the religious leaders and eventually crucified.

Peter now responds with the words "not my feet only but also my hands and my head" The Lord declares "He that is washed does not need washing, save that of his feet (speaking of the walk) but is clean altogether (by the shed blood of Christ) and you are clean, the Lord is speaking of the spiritual not the physical, but adds the words "but not all" referring to Judas Iscariot for He knew who should betray Him. There comes the next revelation to Peter upon his declaration "I will lay down my life for you" but he would deny his Lord three times before the cock should crow.

Self confidence is something advocated by the media on a regular basis so as to obtain the aims and objectives of the individual in his or her pursuit of greatness in the eyes of the people, eliciting much praise and accolade. Unfortunately the element of failure often halts the achievement of such, however it may come. and usually bitter regret and resentment follows. Peter's spirit was to be admired (see Mark ch. 14 v 31), but sadly his actual and real actions were to come short as the Saviour predicted. Who would have thought that the bold, forthright devoted Peter would be so fickle as to deny his Lord in such a way. A salutary warning to all, of the weakness and frailty of human endeavour, when faced with a crisis that challenges our very existence, and loyalty to a person or cause, thus Peter went out and 'wept bitterly' (see Luke ch. 22 v 62) when he remembered the word of the Lord.

The visit of Mary Magdalene to the sepulchre was to reveal that the stone had been taken away, and thinking the worst, she ran to the disciples to inform them and told them, without realising that the Lord had risen, that the body had been stolen. The first to react was Peter, he ran out and came to the sepulchre, with another disciple (possibly John) who outran Peter and came first to the sepulchre.

This disciple did not enter the sepulchre but observed the linen clothes lying, but Peter, on arrival at the sepulchre, went in and saw the linen clothes lying, with the napkin, that was about his head, wrapped together in a place by itself. Then the other disciple went in and saw and believed. Following this discovery the disciples went away again tin their own homes.

After dining Jesus said to Simon Peter "Simon, son of Jonas, Do you love me"? Peter replied "Lord you know I love you "The Lord in reply says "Feed My lambs". A second time the Lord asks "Do you love me", and Peter replies "Lord you know I love you", and again the Saviour says "Feed my sheep". A third time the Saviour asks "Do you love Me", this time Peter was grieved and answers "Lord you know all things, you know that I love you" the Lord replies "Feed my sheep". The Lord then reveals to Peter the future and how he should die saying "Follow Me" (this the Lord said 'twice' – the number of testimony in scripture) as Peter enquired concerning the unnamed disciple and what was to be his lot. This disciple was undoubtedly John, the disciple whom Jesus loved, and he gives true testimony to these things.

When the time and the opportunity, Judas one of the twelve, went before them and drew near to Jesus to kiss Him, but Jesus said to him "Judas, do you betray the Son of Man with a kiss"? John, in his gospel record, tells us of the last supper when Jesus declares "one of you shall betray Me". The response of the disciples was to ask one another, doubting of whom He spoke, and Simon Peter beckoned to John to ask Jesus who it was. The Lord gives the answer indirectly saying "He it is to whom I will give the sop when I have dipped it". When He had dipped the sop He gave it to Judas Iscariot, the son of Simon. Then Satan entered Judas, and Jesus said to Judas, "What you do, do quickly".

Judas knew the place where Jesus often resorted to with His disciples, and came with a band of men and officers from the chief priests and Pharisees, bringing with them lanterns and torches and weapons. Jesus said to them "Whom do you seek"? They answered "Jesus of Nazareth", and the Lord replied "I am He " and Judas stood with them. Upon that declaration of the Lord they all fell backward to the ground, so Jesus asked again "Whom do you seek"?, the answer came "Jesus of Nazareth" Jesus again said "I am He" if you seek Me let these go their way.

Then the band, and the captains and the officers of the Jews Took Jesus and bound Him and Judas was a guide them that took Him.

Then Judas, when he saw that he was condemned, repented himself, andtook the 30 pieces of silver to the chief priests and elders saying "I have sinned in that I have betrayed innocent blood" and they said "what is that to us, you see to it"?, and Judas cast down the pieces of silver, in the temple, and went out and hanged himself. !!! What an end to one who had the privilege and blessing of being part of a company that fellowshipped with the disciples and the Lord himself, and yet did not truly enter the kingdom of God, because his priority was vested in things of this world which were temporal and not eternal.

CHAPTER 13

INDIVIDUAL –
JUDAS ISCARIOT –
JOHN CHAPTERS 13 AND 18

A man highly privileged but chooses to betray the Master for gain.

Influences, from whatever source, often bring an individual into situations and circumstances which, though others may contrive, cause the individual to act either to benefit others or conversely to harm others.

Such was the case with Judas. We are told by John (ch. 13 v 2) that the devil put into the heart of Judas Iscariot, Simon's son, to betray Jesus.

Judas was the treasurer of the company of disciples and was in care of the box, from which he 'pilfered' money for himself, because he was a thief (see John ch. 12 v 6). Money seems to have dominated his thinking and when Mary anointed the Lord, Judas quickly calculated the value of the contents of the jar at three hundred denarii (The amount paid to a labourer for 300 days of work) hence the word of scripture 'very costly'.

Matthew in his gospel account refers to Judas (ch. 10 v 4) when naming the twelve apostles and adds the words 'who also betrayed Him' as does Mark in his account (see Mark ch. 3 v 19) Luke tells us of the arrangement agreed between Judas and the chief priests and captains, how he might betray Him, and they covenanted to give him 'money', and he promised to betray Him in the absence of the multitude (see Luke ch. 27 v's 4 – 6).

CHAPTER 15

INDIVIDUAL – MARY MAGDALENE – MATTHEW CHAPTER 27 VERSE 56; JOHN CHAPTER 19 VERSE 25 & CHAPTER 20 VERSES 1 – 18

A woman devoted to the Lord

Luke tells us that Mary was one of many others who ministered to the Lord out of her substance and out of whom the Saviour had cast 'seven devils'. (demons). Luke also tells she was called Magdalene (see Luke ch. 8 v 2).

Matthew informs us that many women that followed Jesus stood beholding at the cross among whom was Mary Magdalene (see Matthew ch. 27 v's 55 – 56). But it is John who gives us an insight into the devotion of Mary Magdalene, who after the crucifixion, when it was yet dark, arrived at the sepulchre and saw the stone rolled away from the sepulchre.

Her reaction was to run to the disciples (Peter and John) to tell them "They have taken away the Lord, out of the sepulchre and we know not where they have laid Him". Then Peter and John went forth and came to the sepulchre. They ran both together and John did outrun Peter, but did not enter into the sepulchre but stood without, but Peter when he arrived at the sepulchre, went in. Then the disciples went away again to their own homes, but Mary remained outside of the sepulchre weeping, the trauma of recent days and the discovery at the sepulchre was overwhelming causing her to weep unconsolably.

As she wept she stooped down and looked into the sepulchre and saw two angels, one sitting at the head and the other at the feet where the body of Jesus had lain. The angels speak to Mary saying "Why do you weep"? Mary answered "Because they have taken away my Lord and I do not know where they have laid Him". As she said this she turned and saw Jesus. but did not know it was Jesus. Jesus said to her "Woman why are you weeping, who are you seeking"? Mary thought he was the gardener and replied "If you have borne Him hence, tell me where you have laid Him and I will take Him away" Jesus said to her "Mary" and she replied "Rabboni" or "Master". There was something in that voice that registered with Mary and she recognised immediately it was the Lord. The Saviour said to her "Touch Me not for I am not yet ascended to My Father", bur go to My brethren and say to them "I ascend to My Father and your Father and to My God ad your God".

Mary Magdalene went and told the disciples that she had seen the Lord and He had spoken to her. Mark tells us that they did not believe her (see Mark ch. 16 verse 11). John tells us, that the 'same day' at evening, being the 'first day of the week' when the doors were shut where the disciples were gathered, for fear of the Jews, came Jesus and stood in the midst, saying to them, "Peace be to you" and then showed them His hands and His side Then were the disciples glad when 'they saw' the Lord. Then the Lord breathed on them and said "Receive the Holy Ghost".

Again the disciples, at the sea of Tiberias, were given another encounter with the risen Lord when Jesus showed himself to them. Mary of Magdala was uniquely privileged to have an encounter with her Lord. "Go tell My brethren", what joy, what enthusiasm, what excitement filled her soul as she went with the good news that she had seen the Lord and He had spoken to her. Dear soul, have you heard that voice speaking to you, and like the disciples you do not listen or believe; God speaks once, yea twice and man does not comprehend (perceive) (see Job ch. 33 v 14).

CHAPTER 16

I close our consideration of John's characters with a group of individuals of particular interest. Men chosen by the Lord, of various backgrounds, and secular occupation, often weak and unbelieving, but unique and loved by the Saviour.

These characters were part of a group that spent much time with the Saviour, witnessed His unique power, heard His words of Truth, experienced His unconditional love, and recognised His authority as the Son of God.

There are those in this group, who for one reason or another, stand out as a follower of Jesus due to particular events that occurred during the three and a half years of the Lord's ministry, and responded to situations of challenge and responsibility those events brought. Those individuals I have included to teach us that the Lord is no respecter of persons, but can and does use all He calls to Himself, where there is a willingness to be used.

The first is Andrew, Simon Peter's brother. Scripture records that Andrew first finds his brother to bring him the 'good news' we have found 'Messiah' and he brought him to Jesus. Later the Saviour, whilst walking by the sea of Galilee, saw Peter and Andrew casting their net and said to them "Follow Me and I will make you fishers of men" and immediately they left their nets and followed Him. Introduction was followed by invitation and then by initiative (see John ch. 6 v's 8 – 9). It was Andrew who brought the young lad tom the Saviour with the loaves and the fishes. Small things can turn into very large outcomes in the Saviour's hands.

When certain of the Greeks came to see Jesus, it was Philip, who told Andrew and together they came to Jesus. The last mention of Andrew in scripture is in Acts chapter 1 verse 13 where he is named among the eleven apostles an it is recorded 'these all continued with one accord (verse 14). Andrew was no flash in the pan follower of Jesus but a true disciple of the Lord.

Another disciple worthy of mention is Philip, a native of Bethsaida the same city of Andrew and Peter (see John ch. 1 v 44) John tells us Jesus found Philip and said to him "Follow me". Philip then finds Nathanael, to tell him of Jesus from Nazareth, the one of whom Moses and the prophets did write, the son of Joseph. It was later, when Jesus saw Nathanael coming to Him, being brought by Philip, that Jesus revealed His knowledge of Nathanael, eliciting the confession of Nathanael Rabbi you are the Son of God, you are the King of Israel.

It was Philip, who spoke directly to the Lord saying "Show us the Father" Jesus's answer was "Have I been so long a time with you and have you not known Me Philip"? He that has seen Me has seen the Father, Believe Me I am in the Father and the Father in Me or else believe for the very works sake. The statement occurs twice indicating the number of testimony as per requirement of scripture. (In the mouth of two or three witnesses let every word be established).

What Philip is best remembered for is the occasion of the feeding of the five thousand plus, from five loaves and two fishes. The Lord speaking directly to Philip about feeding the large company, "From where shall we buy bread that these may eat"? This the Lord said to him 'to prove him', for the Saviour knew what He himself was going to do. Philip reacted on a natural plane saying, "200 pennyworth is not sufficient for them".

Philip was to witness the power of the Saviour to perform a miracle that was to amaze, not just Philip, but the whole company on that momentous day.

When certain Greeks sought to see Jesus it was Philip who spoke to Andrew and they both approached Jesus. Jesus answered them saying "the hour is come that the Son of Man should be glorified. The declaration of the Lord is apt at this time for He was the 'corn of wheat' and about to die alone, not for the Jews only but also for the Greeks, nay for the whole world (if it die it brings forth much fruit – see John ch3 v 16). It was for the whosoever that Christ died (John ch. 12 v 32)

Among the disciples were two called James, James the brother of John, sons of Zebedee, and James the son of Alphaeus. James the son of Zebedee was among the first to be called by the Lord, whilst he was mending his nets, for he was a fisherman. He at once forsook all and followed the Lord. Both he and his brother were named by the Lord 'Boanerges' ie, 'Sons of thunder' and it was James with John whom asked the Lord if they should call down 'fire from heaven' on the Samaritans (see Luke ch. 9 v 54). The Lord replied "You know not of what manner of spirit you are" for the Son of Man is come not to 'destroy' men's lives but to save them.

These brothers, with Peter, were privileged by the Lord to attend Him on several occasions. In the healing of Jairus's daughter when the company that followed Jesus saw Jeus speaking to Jairus, the ruler of the synagogue, they would have followed Jesus and Jairus, but the Lord suffered no man to follow save Peter, James and John. Thy witnessed not only the laughter of the crowd that had gathered there, but they saw the miracle of the raising of the damsel, for before leaving the house Jairus received news that his daughter was dead.

On another occasion Jesus takes Peter, James and John up an high mountain and was transfigured before them (Matthew ch. 9 v's 2–9). They not only saw the transfiguration of Jesus, but heard the voice of God out of the cloud saying "This is My beloved Son, hear Him".

The same three disciples, with Andrew in tow, asked the Lord in private "What shall be the sign when the temple would be thrown down and the end of the world should be"? The Lord replied with a discourse on events that should take place before He would come to set up the kingdom, exhorting them to watch for no man knows the day or the hour only the Father.

It was at Gethsemane that the Lord took Peter and the two son s of Zebedee (Matthew ch. 26 v 37) with Him as He began to be sorrowful and very heavy. He tells them "My soul is exceeding sorrowful – tarry and watch with Me; when He returns, after being a short distance from them, He finds them sleeping and says to Peter "What, could you not watch with Me one hour"? This situation occurs three times, concluding with the words of the Lord "Sleep on now and take your rest, the spirit is indeed willing but the flesh is weak", were words spoken to Peter on the first of three occasions, that the Lord returned to find them sleeping. How little did they understand of His anticipation in regard to His suffering. How little we, even now. centuries later enter into the suffering He knew.

James, the son of Alphaeus, was not as well known as James, the brother of John, but was an apostle and is named in the list of apostles in the synoptic gospels as well the Acts of the Apostles (ch. 1 v 13). Further mention of him in the book of Acts speaks of a James at Jerusalem who spoke with some authority. Other scriptures seem to indicate that James was active in church matters eg. Acts chapter 12 verse 17, 15 verse

13, 21 verse 18 and Galatians chapter 2 verses 9 & 12. He was probably the writer of the Epistle of Jam es and brother of Jude, who was also an apostle.

The final disciple to be looked at is Thomas (more often known as 'Doubting Thomas') called Didymus, a twin. He is remembered for two significant events. Once, in which, he said to the Lord "we do not know where you are going and how can we know the 'Way'. The Saviour replied with the words" I am the Way, the Truth and the Life (John chapter 14 verses 5 & 6). The other occasion, more well known, when he would not believe that the Lord was risen, but when he saw the Lord he confessed saying.

"My Lord and My God"